THE ANTONINE WALL

THE ANTONINE WALL

DAVID J. BREEZE

HISTORIC SCOTLAND

JOHN DONALD

First published in 2006 by
John Donald, an imprint of Birlinn Ltd

West Newington House
10 Newington Road
Edinburgh
EH9 1QS

www.birlinn.co.uk

ISBN 10: 0 85976 655 1
ISBN 13: 978 0 85976 655 5

British Library Cataloguing-in-Publication Data
A catalogue record for this book is available
from the British Library.

Design: Mark Blackadder

Printed and bound by GraphyCems, Spain

CONTENTS

This distance slab, found at Braidfield, Duntocher, in 1826, records work by soldiers of the Sixth Legion. The plaque recording this is supported by two winged victories.

ACKNOWLEDGEMENTS

I am grateful to Professor A. R. Birley, Dr Brian Dobson, Professor Bill Hanson and Professor Lawrence Keppie for reading and commenting on an earlier draft of this book and to Jackie Henrie for her usual efficient copy editing. I am also grateful to the following for kind permission to reproduce illustrations:

Auld Kirk Museum, Kirkintilloch 10.4, 10.5; The British Library 2.4; © The Trustees of the British Museum 1.1; Deutsche Limes-kommission 4.9, 5.3, 11.2; Falkirk Museum 7.7; Historic Scotland 2.8, 2.12, 4.1, 4.3, 5.2, 5.6, 5.8, 5.9, 5.10, 5.12, 5.13, 5.14, 5.16, 5.18, 5.19, 5.21, 6.1, 6.3, 6.4, 6.6, 6.9, 6.10, 6.12, 6.13, 6.14, 7.1, 7.3, 8.1, 8.3, 8.4, 8.5, 8.6, 9.4, 10.1, 10.2, 10.7, A.1, A.2, A.3; Hunterian Museum and Art Gallery, University of Glasgow page VI, 1.4, 1.5, 1.7, 2.1, 5.7, 5.22, 6.8, 7.4, 7.5, 7.6, 7.10, 9.3, 11.1, A.4; Angus Lamb 3.2, 4.6, 4.7, 6.15, 8.2, 8.6; the Trustees of the National Galleries of Scotland 10.3; National Library of Scotland 2.5; the Trustees of the National Museums of Scotland 2.3, 4.4, 4.8, 5.4, 7.8, 7.9, 9.2; Ordinance Survey 4.5; Römisch-Germanischen Zentral-museum, Mainz 3.1, 3.3; Royal Commission on the Ancient and Historical Monuments of Scotland 2.10, 4.9, 5.5, 6.2, 6.5; Society of Antiquaries of London 2.6, 2.7; Society of Antiquaries of Scotland 7.2; Vindolanda Trust 6.7. All other photographs are my own. I am further grateful to my colleagues Bryony Coombs and David Henrie for much help with the illustrations.

MEASUREMENTS

All measurements are given in metric with imperial in brackets. Where appropriate, Roman measurements are also provided. A straight translation from imperial to metric can sometimes be misleading as the original measurements were often not as precise as a detailed metric figure can imply. Some latitude has therefore been allowed, for example when 'yards' have been used to indicate an approximate distance. Metric measurements are given to the second decimal point, except where this detail has not been provided in the original excavation report.

One Roman mile (*mille passuum*, that is 1,000 paces, one pace being 2 steps of 5 Roman feet) = 1,618 yards = 1,479 m

One Roman foot = 11.64 imperial inches = 296 mm

INTRODUCTION

If a man were called to fix the period in the history of the world,
during which the condition of the human race was most happy and
prosperous, he would, without hesitation, name that which elapsed
from the death of Domitian to the accession of Commodus.

EDWARD GIBBON,
The Decline and Fall of the Roman Empire (London 1776)

A Roman state existed in one form or another for over 2,000 years. The traditional date for the foundation of Rome was 753 BC while Constantinople fell to the Turks in AD 1453. The empire of the Roman state grew slowly, but by the middle of the second century AD it completely encircled the Mediterranean Sea – *Mare Nostrum*, Our Sea – and included all or part of over thirty modern countries. It stretched for over 2,500 miles west to east from the Atlantic Ocean to modern Iraq, and for nearly 2,000 miles north to south from the Highlands of Scotland to the Sahara Desert.

Once aggressively expansionist, by the second century AD that process had slowed down. The Emperor Trajan (97–117) conquered Dacia and Parthia, but the new provinces in the east were abandoned by his successor Hadrian (117–38) and thereafter, with the exception of the Eastern conquests of Septimius Severus (193–211), there were to be no major new additions, though it was to be another 150 years before the contraction of the empire began. As the expansion slowed,

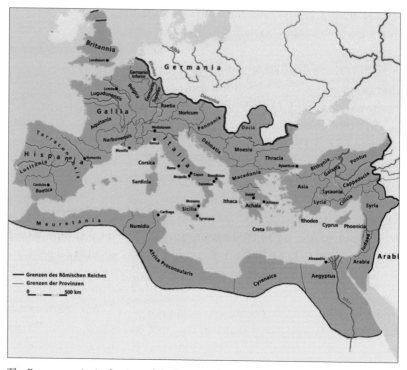

The Roman empire in the time of the Emperor Antoninus Pius.

the Romans started to construct frontiers to define and protect their empire. The process had begun by the late first century and reached its apogee with the building of the Antonine Wall in Scotland in the 140s. For a single generation, from 142 to the early 160s, the Antonine Wall stood as the north-west frontier of the Roman empire before, for a reason which we still do not know, it was abandoned.

The Antonine Wall is one of only three artificial frontiers built by the Romans to protect their European provinces. The others are Hadrian's Wall and the German *limes*. Elsewhere, in Dacia (modern Romania) and in north Africa, shorter lengths of bank and ditch, or stone wall, were used to control access to the empire but they are not as well explored and dated as the frontiers of north-west Europe. Enough is known, however, to indicate that these linear barriers owed their origins to Hadrian.

Hadrian's Wall was declared a World Heritage Site in 1987. Ten years later, Germany started the long process to have their frontier ascribed as a World Heritage Site, succeeding in July 2005 when it was formally added to the list of about 800 Sites by UNESCO. At that point a new type of World Heritage Site came into existence, a multi-national Site, for UNESCO had decided not to elevate each section of the Roman frontier within each modern country to the status of a separate World Heritage Site, but to create a single Site embracing all sections of the frontier and all modern countries. This new World Heritage Site is called *Frontiers of the Roman Empire*, and, so far, consists of Hadrian's Wall and the German *limes*. However, already several countries have announced their intention to nominate their sections of the frontier as part of this new World Heritage Site. These countries are Austria, Slovakia, Hungary, Croatia and the UK for the Antonine Wall.

In January 2003, the then Deputy Minister for Culture and Sport in Scotland, Dr Elaine Murray, announced that the Scottish Executive intended to nominate the Antonine Wall as a World Heritage Site. Preparations began immediately. Officials of Historic Scotland and all five of the local councils which include the Antonine Wall in their areas – East Dunbartonshire, Falkirk, Glasgow, North Lanarkshire and West Dunbartonshire – are working closely to ensure that all necessary protective measures are in place and that a protective buffer zone for the monument is defined. These are two of the measures required by UNESCO. The potential World Heritage Site also needs to be defined in map form. The Royal Commission on the Ancient and Historical Monuments of Scotland is preparing a new map which brings together the results of survey and excavation along the Antonine Wall over the last 250 years, and provides, through GIS and its own electronically-based archive, a tool for its better management – a further requirement of UNESCO.

There have been other initiatives in relation to the proposals. Mrs Patricia Ferguson, Minister for Tourism, Culture and Sport, subsequently announced an education initiative in 2004. The aim is to see how schools might want to use the Antonine Wall in their teaching – in Chinese schools, World Heritage Sites are used as a vehicle for teaching modern citizenship. A booklet providing information on the nomination of the Antonine Wall was launched in 2004, and a second publication on the wider proposal to create a new Frontiers of the Roman Empire World Heritage Site in 2005.

The purpose of this book is to provide an account of the Antonine Wall. The aim, however, is not just to describe the Wall, but to place it in its British and Roman imperial setting and consider its importance and significance. From one perspective, the Antonine Wall was a 'normal' frontier containing many features found elsewhere. From another, it has many unique or unusual elements. These include aspects of the structure itself. This, not unusually, was of turf, but it was uniquely erected on a stone base. The forts were closer together than on any other frontier and many had associated annexes. No annexes appear on Hadrian's Wall and they are rare on the German frontier. In addition, there were 'expansions', probably serving as beacon-platforms, and small enclosures, unfortunately of unknown purpose, both unparalled on any other frontier. Many camps are known along the line of Hadrian's Wall, but the long life of that frontier renders it difficult to distinguish between labour, marching and practice camps. The short life of the Antonine Wall allows us to see that most camps were constructed and used by the soldiers building the frontier. The distribution of these camps enables us to understand something of the process of building the frontier. Relating the camps to the surviving distance slabs provides another level of understanding about the division of labour. These distance slabs, of which twenty are known either whole or in part, record the lengths of Wall built by each of the three legions involved in the work. They are not, though, simple records, but highly decorated and sculptured stones which depict events and form the single most important collection of Roman military sculpture from any frontier of the Roman empire. They are a most significant element of Scotland's historical heritage, as is the Antonine Wall itself.

The Antonine Wall was the most complex and highly developed of all frontiers constructed by the Roman army. It lay at the end of a development process which had started sixty years earlier in Britain and much earlier on the Continent. Following its abandonment, the army was never again to build such a complex frontier system, thus the Antonine Wall stands alone amongst all Roman frontiers. Its special position appears to have been recognised at the time for the distance slabs which record its construction and represent a brazen statement of imperialist aggression are a unique testimony on any frontier to the power and might of Rome.

The application to have the Antonine Wall added to the Frontiers of the Roman Empire World Heritage Site will not be decided until 2007–8. In the meantime, I hope that this book will provide information about a monument which can still be seen and explored today and which for twenty years was the north-west frontier of one of the world's greatest states.

This book is not a detailed academic treatise about the Antonine Wall, nor is it a guide-book. Gordon Maxwell and Bill Hanson's *Rome's North-West Frontier: The Antonine Wall* (Edinburgh 1986) is still the most comprehensive and detailed modern account of the Wall, while the guide-book by Anne Robertson and Lawrence Keppie, *The Antonine Wall, A Handbook to the Surviving Remains* (Glasgow 2001) is indispensable for those wishing to follow the Wall on the ground: it also contains an up-to-date and full bibliography. The aim of this book is to bring together the results of recent research and offer an account of the Antonine Wall and the man who ordered its construction.

Fig. 1.1 Antoninus Pius.

ANTONINUS PIUS

Antoninus never willingly made war ...

PAUSANIAS,
Description of Greece, 8, 43

On 10 July 138, the Roman empire acquired a new ruler. On that day, the Emperor Hadrian died in his villa at Baiae on the bay of Naples and was succeeded peacefully by his chosen successor, the man known to history as Antoninus Pius. The reign of the new emperor over the whole empire was to last longer than any other of his predecessors or successors with the exception of the founder of the empire, Augustus. Yet, he is relatively little known and the reasons for his two expansions of the empire – in Britain and in Germany – remain a matter of conjecture. Partly, this results from a lack of contemporary sources – the only biography of Antoninus was written 200 years after his death. Yet, this was Gibbon's Golden Age when the deeds of Antoninus' immediate predecessors, Trajan and Hadrian, and his successor, Marcus Aurelius, are well known. Who was this man who controlled the destiny of millions of people for twenty-three years and, in Scotland, ordered the construction of the Antonine Wall?

TITUS AURELIUS ANTONINUS

The new emperor was born Titus Aurelius Fulvus Boionius Arrius

Antoninus at Lanuvium a little to the south of Rome on 19 September 86. He was the only child of Titus Aurelius Fulvus and Arria Fadilla. His father was consul in 89, and his father, T. Aurelius Fulvus from Nîmes in Gallia Narbonensis (Provence), consul before him. Indeed, as his other grandfather had also been a consul, Antoninus had a distinguished background. Yet, the family had only recently risen into the top echelons of society, gaining advancement as a result of the disturbances which followed the death of the Emperor Nero in 68 when four emperors ruled in quick succession.

The family had two estates close to Rome, at Lanuvium and at Lorium. Antoninus was brought up and educated at Lorium, 20 km (12 miles) to the west of Rome, which he always regarded as his home. About 110 he married Annia Galeria Faustina, daughter of Marcus Annius Verus and Rupilia Faustina. Annius Verus was to have the rare distinction of being consul three times. There were two sons of the marriage, who both died young, and two daughters.

Antoninus was very wealthy, owning much property in Etruria and Umbria. Two hundred years later, his biographer was to offer a thumbnail sketch: 'He was a man of striking appearance, his natural capacities were brilliant and his character kindly. His countenance was noble, his innate qualities were outstanding – he was a polished speaker and exceptionally learned. A man of moderation and a thrifty landowner, of mild disposition, with his own he was generous and he kept away from what belonged to others. All these qualities were in balance and without ostentation.' According to one story, he gained the surname Pius because of his solicitude for his aged father-in-law Annius Verus; another that it reflected his respect for his predecessor; while a third suggested that the Senate granted the title to acknowledge his devotion to the gods.

Many aristocrats like Antoninus followed a career in the emperor's service, holding a succession of senior military and civilian posts in Rome and the provinces, in effect helping to run the empire. This clearly did not appeal to Antoninus. He held the basic posts, serving as quaestor and praetor, before becoming consul in 120. Subsequently he only held two senior posts, both very prestigious and presumably held for that reason. He served as governor of one of the four provinces created by Hadrian in Italy and was proconsul of Asia in 134–5. Yet, while his interests did not lie in the direction of public service, he did serve on the emperor's council.

IMPERATOR TITUS AELIUS AURELIUS CAESAR ANTONINUS

The Emperor Hadrian had no children and in 136 made arrangements for the succession. He chose, for reasons which are unclear, Lucius Ceionius Commodus. The new Caesar was only in his thirties, but not a fit man, and Hadrian's intention may have been that he should merely be a stand-in until his real preference, Marcus Aurelius, was old enough to succeed. However, the emperor's plans were thwarted by the death of his nominee on 1 January 138. Later that month, Hadrian announced the name of his new choice as successor, the 51-year-old Titus Aurelius Antoninus. Antoninus did not accept immediately, but on 25 February he was formally adopted by Hadrian and invested with appropriate powers. His new name was Imperator Titus Aelius Aurelius Caesar Antoninus.

Several reasons may have led to the choice of Antoninus. Firstly, he was clearly a man of peace. He had no military experience and presumably Hadrian thought that at fifty-one he was unlikely to undertake new military adventures and therefore reverse Hadrian's own policies which had been resolutely non-expansionist. Secondly, Antoninus was popular, mild-mannered and a respected adminis-trator. Hadrian, in the speech put into his mouth by Cassius Dio, described him as '… noble, mild, compassionate and prudent. He is neither young enough to do anything rash nor old enough to be neglectful. He has exercised authority in accordance with our ancestral customs, so that he is not ignorant of any matters which concern the imperial power, but he can deal with them all. I know that he is not in the least inclined to be involved in affairs and is far from desiring such power.' Finally, Antoninus may have been distantly related to Hadrian through his father-in-law Annius Verus, but, more importantly, he was the uncle by marriage of Marcus Aurelius.

Hadrian had come to know Marcus and was impressed by him.

Fig. 1.2 The Castel Sant'Angelo on the west bank of the River Tiber in Rome was built as a mausoleum by Hadrian, being completed by Antoninus. However, it acquired the name, *Antoninorum sepulcrum*, the burial place of the Antonines.

As a result, he had taken an interest in the boy's education. All our information points to the fact that Hadrian saw the young Marcus – at present only fourteen – as his eventual heir and Lucius Ceionius Commodus and Antoninus were merely place-men until the boy was old enough to succeed. However, he badly miscalculated in both cases for Commodus died too early and Antoninus, although only ten years younger than Hadrian, was to live for another twenty-three years!

Antoninus' first task was to cremate Hadrian and bury his ashes. Antoninus had been with Hadrian when he died at Baiae. He now buried his predecessor at Cicero's former villa at Puteoli, a short distance from Baiae, and erected a temple there. The new emperor then travelled to Rome to persuade the Senate to deify Hadrian and approve all his acts. This was a most difficult task as Hadrian was hated by the Senate. Nevertheless, Antoninus achieved this delicate mission, though he had to agree to abolish the four consular posts established by Hadrian to govern Italy.

Antoninus also had to complete the construction of Hadrian's great new mausoleum, built across the River Tiber from the mausoleum of Augustus which was now full. This was achieved in 139 and Hadrian's ashes were then brought to Rome and placed, together with those of his wife, in the new mausoleum which is known today as Castel Sant' Angelo. They were joined by the ashes of Antoninus' two sons and his daughter and then by those of other members of his family and his successors down to Septimius Severus, his wife and his sons in the early third century.

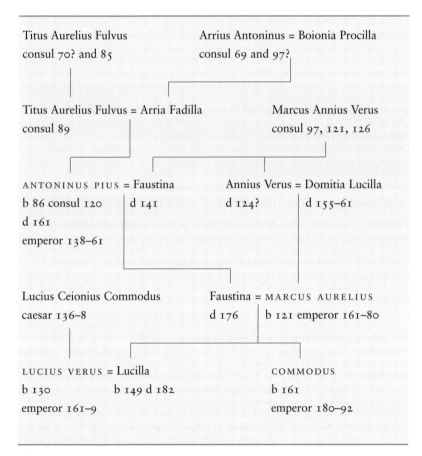

Titus Aurelius Fulvus consul 70? and 85		Arrius Antoninus = Boionia Procilla consul 69 and 97?	

Titus Aurelius Fulvus = Arria Fadilla
consul 89

Marcus Annius Verus
consul 97, 121, 126

ANTONINUS PIUS = Faustina
b 86 consul 120   d 141
d 161
emperor 138–61

Annius Verus = Domitia Lucilla
d 124?   d 155–61

Lucius Ceionius Commodus
caesar 136–8

Faustina = MARCUS AURELIUS
d 176   b 121 emperor 161–80

LUCIUS VERUS = Lucilla
b 130   b 149 d 182
emperor 161–9

COMMODUS
b 161
emperor 180–92

Table 1 The family of Antoninus Pius

Our knowledge of Antoninus' reign is based upon his much later biography, some inscriptions, citations of his judgements in law books and brief comments by contemporaries. It would appear that his internal policy was broadly conservative. He consulted his council before any action and was accessible to petitioners. He ensured that taxation, government administration and judicial procedures were fair: among the laws he enforced were those against the maltreatment of slaves. He is known to have left a considerable body of legislation. He erected few new buildings in Rome, preferring to complete Hadrian's or repair existing structures, but he supported new building works in Italy and the provinces. These included harbours, roads and bridges, all contributing to an improved economy. He responded positively to disasters such as earthquakes, famines, floods and fires; one fire in Rome during his reign destroyed 340 blocks of houses. As a result, states his biographer, the provinces all flourished under him. He lived off his own income and on his own private estates but not in an ostentatious way that would excite criticism. He did not travel, ostensibly so as to not burden the provincials with the cost of looking after the imperial retinue. According to Cassius Dio, he left 675 million *denarii* in the Treasury at his death.

As his adopted son, son-in-law and chosen successor, Marcus Aurelius, grew older, Antoninus shared power with him. In 147 Marcus Aurelius was given powers almost equal to those of the emperor himself and for the remaining thirteen years of his reign the two were virtually co-emperors.

Antoninus undertook those actions expected of a Roman emperor. He gave spectacular public games in Rome at which many animals were slaughtered; and he repaired the Circus Maximus following a structural collapse. He gave money to the people of Rome and to the army. In 147/8 the 900th anniversary of the founding of Rome was celebrated, and the opportunity was taken to commemorate the men who had made Rome great: Aeneas, Romulus, Numa Pompilius and Augustus. Antoninus supported the conservative values of Rome and this is underlined by his coinage which reflected the religious traditions which he and his fellow Romans believed had helped to make their state great.

Fig. 1.3 The temple erected by Antoninus Pius to his wife Faustina in the Forum in Rome was turned into a church, St Lawrence, during the Middle Ages.

If by disposition he reflected the traditional values of Rome, his tastes also acknowledged the eclectic nature of his inheritance. Both he and his wife were followers of the goddess Cybele. Worshippers, offered salvation after their earthly labours, indulged in hysterical and orgiastic pageants and ceremonies at which bulls were killed. The animals' blood poured over the bodies of the initiates, who were in pits below the sacrifice, thereby bestowing upon them rebirth. One of the centres of the cult was Lanuvium, birthplace of Antoninus.

In some ways, he rejected the style of his immediate predecessors, not indulging in grandiose wars of conquest like Trajan or foreign travels like Hadrian.

FOREIGN POLICY

The traditional values espoused by Antoninus were very necessary, for his reign was not entirely peaceful. His reign saw military action of various degrees of seriousness on all three frontiers of the empire – on the northern frontier in Britain and Germany, on the Black Sea coast, in the Caucusus and in Mauretania – and diplomatic action also in the East and on the northern frontier in central Europe. In addition, there were rebellions in at least three provinces, Egypt, Greece and Dacia, while, in an obscure incident, Cornelius Priscianus was condemned by the Senate for 'disturbing the peace of the province of Spain in a hostile manner'.

At the beginning of his reign, Antoninus pushed forward the frontier in Britain, an event to which we will return. Towards the end of his reign he was to undertake a similar action in Germany. Although we do not know the reason for this latter move forward, it brought into the empire rich farmland which had been under Roman surveillance for about seventy years and established the new frontier line on the edge of the Black Forest which was largely uninhabited. It could be seen therefore as a tidying-up operation. Little is known of actions elsewhere on the European frontier at this time, though a coin of 140–44 does record Antoninus giving a king to the Quadi, who inhabited modern Slovakia.

139–42	Reconquest of southern Scotland and construction of Antonine Wall
142/3	Trouble with Getae, Libyans and around the Red Sea
140–44	Gives a king to the Armenians
140–44	Gives a king to the Quadi
early in reign?	Pharasmanes, king of Iberia in the Caucusus, visits Rome
145–50	Warfare in Numidia and Mauretania
148	The new king of Parthia, Vologases IV, threatens Rome
151–5	Special command in Germany may indicate trouble from the Chatti
154	Rebellion in Egypt
156/7–8	Rebellion in Dacia
159/61	Parthian war threatened
late 150s	Advance in Germany and construction of new frontier

Table 2 Foreign affairs

Mauretania and Numidia in north Africa suffered from the depredations of brigands, who were probably raiders from beyond the empire. In 145 a legionary detachment was sent from Judaea but success there was followed by more serious warfare in Mauretania. Reinforcements had to be sent from many of the European provinces, probably including Britain, and it was at least four years before order was restored. An uprising in Upper Egypt occurred shortly after, and then a revolt in Dacia, quelled by Statius Priscus who was later to be governor of Britain. Antoninus' biographer also records a rebellion in Greece. Aelius Aristides in his speech in honour of Rome, delivered before the imperial court probably in 142 or 143, mentions 'trouble with the Getae, the Libyans and the people round the Red Sea'.

Antoninus inherited a volatile situation in the far north-east corner of his domain. The Alani, who lived between the Black Sea and the Caspian Sea north of the Caucasus, encouraged by Pharasmanes, king of Iberia to the south, invaded their neighbours and pushed on southwards to threaten both the Roman province of Cappadocia and the northern border of Parthia: this was probably in

Fig. 1.4 Coin of Antoninus Pius bearing the legend REX ARMENIIS DATUS, a king given to the Armenians.

136. Flavius Arrianus, governor of Cappadocia, took to the field with a powerful force and the Alani withdrew. The Parthians, annoyed at the action of Pharasmanes, a Roman client, sent an embassy to Rome to complain. Early in the reign of Antoninus, Pharasmanes and his family travelled to Rome and were well received, being allowed to make a sacrifice on the Capitol. While flattery was the treatment offered to Rome's client, the Alani continued to be troublesome and Antoninus had to undertake further action against them, though we do not know the nature of this. It is possible that his appointment of Pacorus to be king of the Lazi, a client state on the eastern shore of the Black Sea, was part of his attempt to curtail the activities of the Alani.

A major test for any emperor in the field of foreign affairs was the relationship with the Parthian empire on the Eastern frontier. This was the only state of equivalent power and a wrong or casual action could have terrible consequences. Here, Antoninus followed a strong line, towards the beginning of his reign giving a king to the Armenians and later dealing firmly with the new king of Parthia, Vologases IV, who had designs on Armenia. Nevertheless, an inscription records that Neratius Proculus was sent to Syria with detachments 'for the Parthian war', though fighting does not appear to have broken out.

Whenever possible, Antoninus relied upon diplomacy. When Abgar king of Edessa on the Eastern frontier attacked one of his neighbours, a letter from Antoninus was sufficient to bring him into line. He dealt with several disputes amongst the royal families of the kingdoms of the area, including that of the Bosphoran kingdom of the Crimea. Yet when the neighbouring city of Olbia, situated on the north shore of the Black Sea between the Crimea and Lower Moesia, was attacked by Scythians, he sent a force of auxiliaries to support Rome's client and help defeat the aggressors.

These wars and the acquisition of new territory stand in complete contrast to the statement by Pausanias that 'Antoninus never willingly waged war'. Of course, from the Roman perspective, that may be true: the Romans were forced into war by the actions of their neighbours. Nevertheless, the assertion that Antoninus was a man of peace does chime well with several statements of the time.

It was during the reign of Antoninus that Appian started to write his *History of Rome*. He wrote, '... in general, possessing by good government the most important parts of land and sea, they prefer to preserve their empire rather than extend it indefinitely to poor and profitless barbarian peoples. I have seen embassies from some of these in Rome offering themselves as subjects, and the emperor refusing them, on the grounds that they would be of no use to him. For other peoples, limitless in number, the emperors appoint the kings, not requiring them for the empire.... They surround the empire with a circle of great camps and guard so great an area of land and sea like an estate.'

At the same time, Aelius Aristides wrote in his *Roman Oration* of the walls which the Romans had placed round their empire, 'an encamped army like a rampart encloses the civilised world in a ring'.

In these three writers – Pausanias, Appian and Aelius Aristides – we perhaps see the official governmental line: the Romans were content with what they had. Or perhaps these statements were simply a justification for current imperial policy, which could – and was – reversed at will. Appian and Aelius Aristides, we should note, were Greek, with a very different view of empire from the imperialistic Romans. Furthermore, within the second century, the views of

Hadrian and Antoninus were at variance both with the actions of their predecessor Trajan and of their successors. Marcus Aurelius (161–80), it appears, intended to deal with the incipient warfare on his northern frontier by creating two new provinces beyond the Danube, while Septimius Severus (193–211) was responsible for extending the frontier in the east, south and north-west. It was clearly still possible to think of the empire continuing to expand. If the expansionist view was not always predominant, it was partly because the balance was tipping against the Romans.

BRITAIN

It is all the more surprising within the nature of his inheritance and the spirit of his times that Antoninus should opt for a forward movement in Britain. There can be no doubt that this was one of the early decisions of his reign. An inscription erected at Corbridge records the construction of a building by the army under the governor Quintus Lollius Urbicus in 139. Corbridge lies on Dere Street, just south of Hadrian's Wall, and activity there can often be connected either with wider changes along Hadrian's Wall or with activities in Scotland. In this case, Scotland seems the more likely as Urbicus was the new governor sent to Britain by Antoninus. The *Life of Antoninus Pius* records this in the following way: 'He [Antoninus] conquered Britain through his legate Lollius Urbicus, and, having driven back the barbarians, built a new wall, this time of turf'. Hadrian had died in July 138, too late in the season for action that year, so 139 was the earliest opportunity for a new policy to become visible.

This action in Britain, occurring at the very beginning of the reign of Antoninus, and resulting in the abandonment of Hadrian's Wall, perhaps the greatest physical expression of that emperor's frontier policy, was the only occasion after his accession that the new emperor took the title *Imperator*, Conqueror. While there may have been trouble on the northern British frontier at the time – the travel writer Pausanias mentions an insurrection in northern Britain during the reign – there is no doubt that the army could have dealt with this without the need to move the frontier 150 km (100 miles) to the north. It has been suggested that the purpose of the northwards move of the frontier was to place the Roman army in a better position to deal with the main enemy in the north, the Caledonians. However, they could be controlled by treaty, as indeed they probably were most of the time. If there was no major problem in Britain which necessitated abandoning one frontier and building another, then perhaps the move north was related to Antoninus' own position.

In choosing a man of peace, Hadrian created something of a problem for his successor. The Roman empire was not a constitutional monarchy; rather it was a military dictatorship. Power, in the end, depended upon the support of the army, though the senators in Rome were also important – during the first two centuries of the Roman empire more emperors perished as a result of palace intrigues than military action. Antoninus had no military experience and it is possible that he considered that his authority would be increased by winning a short war. Exactly 100 years before, another new emperor, Claudius, required a triumph, according to the Roman biographer Suetonius, and he chose Britain as the place to win his military prestige. Perhaps Antoninus followed the same pattern of thought. Certainly, the fact that he did not take the title *Imperator* again in spite of his other victories is most suggestive.

Whatever the reason for the advance north, we can be sure that the situation in Britain was a minor concern to the new emperor and his advisors. It has been suggested that Antoninus may have considered it politic to abandon Hadrian's Wall and conquer new territory to placate Trajan's marshals, still powerful in Rome yet rendered inactive by Hadrian's pacific frontier policy. Perhaps the abandonment of Hadrian's Wall was a sop thrown to the senators who were proving difficult to persuade to honour Hadrian's memory in an appropriate manner. It is doubtful if many in Rome, who must have had only the haziest appreciation of the location and nature of Hadrian's Wall, would have spoken in favour of retaining a frontier work erected by the hated emperor. But neither suggestion can be proved and both are less likely than the simple solution that Antoninus required a triumph.

It is interesting, too, that the move north was limited in scope. This was not an attempt to complete the conquest of the island and remove the necessity for there being a frontier in Britain. It was a very short step forward, 'conquering' territory which had once been Roman and, we might expect, had been kept under Roman surveillance ever since.

There is one other reference which supports the theory that the advance related to Antoninus' own position. At the close of the British war, Cornelius Fronto, tutor to Marcus Aurelius, gave a speech congratulating the emperor on his success. Almost certainly this speech was delivered in the Senate when he was consul, which was in 142. Fronto declared that 'although he [Antoninus] had committed the conduct of the campaign to others, while sitting at home himself in the Palace at Rome [= the Palatine], yet like the helmsman at the tiller of a ship of war, the glory of the whole navigation and voyage belonged to him'. This may simply be extravagant praise, but it also may contain a hint – a strong hint – that this war was special and important for the emperor.

If the aim of the British war was to gain military prestige, it seems to have worked. Antoninus was troubled by no internal military disturbances: his army remained loyal and he died in his bed twenty years later. It may seem strange to us that the Antonine Wall was constructed merely in order to bolster the authority of an emperor over 1,000 miles away in Rome, but stranger things have happened in the world of politics.

DECISION MAKING

The British war and the construction of the Antonine Wall have so far been seen as effectively the decision of the emperor. While this is certainly true, the biographer of Antoninus emphasised that before he took important decisions the emperor consulted his council. What was this council?

There are many records of emperors consulting their 'friends' (*amici*). While a formal Cabinet or Privy Council as such did not exist in the Roman state, it is clear that sensible emperors always sought advice from their senior officials, relatives and experienced senior senators. Two men who had married into the family of Antoninus were known to have served on his council.

Among the senior officials was the praetorian prefect: there were two at the beginning of the reign, one serving for nearly twenty years in the post. The praetorian prefect was a man of wide experience, holding the most senior position in the army and, most importantly, commanding the garrison of Rome. A second military man on the council was the prefect of the city of Rome. In the latter part of the reign of Antoninus this was Lollius Urbicus, the former governor of Britain. It is possible that he too held his post for many years, since one prefect died in 146 and another, possibly Urbicus, in 160: perhaps he held the position throughout these fourteen years.

Another official in the emperor's council was the secretary for correspondence. During the early years of Hadrian's reign this post was held by the biographer Suetonius, who accompanied the emperor to Britain in 122. Nearly a hundred years later, another historian, Cassius Dio, was the 'friend' of three emperors, Septimius Severus, Caracalla and Severus Alexander.

A well-known member of the imperial court was Cornelius Fronto. A native of Cirta in north Africa, like Lollius Urbicus, he was the pre-eminent man of letters in Rome from the reign of Hadrian to that of Marcus Aurelius. He was a senator and an advocate in the law courts of Rome. Most importantly, he was tutor to the young Marcus. His surviving letters offer an insight into intrigues and feuds present even within the court of the utterly respectable Antoninus Pius.

The emperor might also consult those with specialist knowledge. We know that in the autumn of 140 Antoninus and Marcus Aurelius visited Pompeius Falco, governor of Britain at the beginning of Hadrian's reign. Possibly others who had served on the island were consulted.

Marcus Aurelius in his *Meditations* remarked that Antoninus formed his views carefully after searching and persistent discussion; he

Fig. 1.5 Coin of Antoninus Pius showing his funeral pyre.

Fig. 1.6 The base of the column dedicated to Antoninus Pius and erected in the Campus Martius, Rome, beside the funeral pyre of the emperor. In effect it is a cenotaph. On one side is the apotheosis of Antoninus Pius and Faustina. This scene is flanked on two other faces by soldiers in funeral processions.

Fig. 1.7 Coin of Antoninus Pius showing the column erected in his honour in Rome.

then held to them firmly. It was these firm views that would have been communicated to Lollius Urbicus before his departure for Britain.

As Urbicus was governor of Lower Germany and did not return to Rome before crossing the Channel to Britain, his instructions would have been written down and sent to him. In return, Urbicus would have been expected to report back to the emperor regularly, as Tacitus records his father-in-law Agricola doing when he was governor of Britain. Personal relations and the personal grant of authority were very important in the Roman world. When an emperor died, the authority given to his officers died with him, and they had to seek instructions from the new emperor. Urbicus was in the fortunate position that this did not happen to him, but we can be sure that he appreciated the special relationship he had with the man who was directing his actions.

THE DEATH OF ANTONINUS

In many ways, the long reign of Antoninus Pius was the lull before the storm. He died on 7 March 161 in his seventy-fifth year at his childhood home of Lorium after being emperor for twenty-two years and nine months. He was cremated on the Campus Martius in Rome and his ashes placed with those of other members of his family in the

Mausoleum of Hadrian – Castel Sant'Angelo. A column was erected beside the funeral pyre by his adopted sons and successors, Lucius Verus and Marcus Aurelius. This was rediscovered in the early eighteenth century, but today only the base survives and is preserved in the Vatican Gardens.

The reigns of his successors were largely taken up by warfare on distant frontiers. They had not been prepared for such events. Although they had been provided with the normal education of the aristocracy, it had been confined to Rome. Antoninus had not sought fit to introduce them to the wider experience of service in the provinces, either in civil or military posts.

A year after the death of Antoninus, Lucius left Rome for the East where the king of Parthia, long held in check by Antoninus, had invaded and conquered Armenia. The war was to last four years. It was no sooner over than there was an invasion of the northern frontier in Pannonia (modern Austria and Hungary). Although the initial attack was repulsed, it was followed by more and as a result Marcus was to spend many campaigning seasons in the Danube region: he died there, in Vienna, in 180.

Antoninus' careful husbanding of the empire's resources helped to ensure peace and prosperity. His skilful diplomacy appears to have ensured the maintenance of Roman power along her frontiers during his lifetime. We can only presume that this habitual care was also extended to Britain.

II

SOURCES

Antoninus conquered Britain through his legate
Lollius Urbicus, and, having driven back the barbarians,
built a new wall, this time of turf.

HISTORIA AUGUSTA,
Life of Antoninus, 5, 4

Our knowledge of both internal and foreign affairs during the reign of Antoninus Pius is so poor simply because of the paucity of the literary evidence. His *Life*, written 200 years later, is relatively brief, especially on foreign and frontiers policy and is excessively laudatory. Reading the few pages today, it appears that the emperor was a paragon of virtue: kindly, learned, moderate, thrifty, generous, merciful, dignified, private in his habits yet well-known .... Perhaps he was, but it would be helpful to have corroborative evidence. It is especially unfortunate that this section of Cassius Dio's *History of Rome* is lost. The few references to Antoninus in the letters of Cornelius Fronto and the *Meditations* of Marcus Aurelius are hardly unbiased sources.

Other sources only provide details. Two coin issues tell us that he gave kings to the Armenians and the Quadi: REX ARMENIIS DATVS and REX QUADIS DATVS. Both date to between his third and fourth consulates, 140–4. His legal rulings are preserved in inscriptions and later compilations of Roman law, while inscriptions also record his support of public works and buildings.

Fig. 2.1 Coin of Antoninus Pius issued in 143 in celebration of the victory in Britain. On the reverse it shows the goddess Victory and BRITAN.

LITERARY DOCUMENTS AND BUILDING INSCRIPTIONS

We are fortunate in possessing nearly twenty building inscriptions from the Antonine Wall which specifically include the name of Antoninus, twice the number from Hadrian's Wall which record the name of its builder: by comparison, hardly any survive from the German frontier.

We have already examined the literary sources for the building of the Antonine Wall. These consist of the statement that Lollius Urbicus conquered Britain and built a new wall, of turf, and that the emperor directed the war from his palace in Rome. Two military diplomas issued on 1 August 142 record that Antoninus had been acclaimed *Imperator* for the second time – that is, for his victory in Britain – by that date. A coin issue of late 142 or early 143 bears the figure of *Britannia* and the legend IMPERATOR II on the reverse. If Fronto's speech was indeed delivered when he was consul in 142, this would provide further evidence that the victory had been achieved by that year. Perhaps the campaigning was restricted to 140 and 141.

Inscriptions from the British frontier provide further information about the activities of Lollius Urbicus. Two inscribed stones at Corbridge on Dere Street record building activity under the

Fig. 2.2 This building inscription records the erection of a building at Corbridge in the second consulship of Antoninus Pius, that is in 139, and during the governorship of Quintus Lollius Urbicus, by the Second Legion Augusta.

governor, one dating to 139. He is also recorded on two building inscriptions at the fort of Balmuildy on the Antonine Wall, and on one at High Rochester, also on Dere Street.

The events of the governorship are therefore clear. Urbicus was already in Britain in 139, the summer after the accession of Antoninus, and had started his preparations for the reconquest of southern Scotland by remodelling the base at Corbridge on one of the arterial roads to the north. Victory had been achieved by 142 and before the governor left, probably the same year, a start had been made on the construction of the Antonine Wall and its attendant forts.

These sources make sense, but there is one other which does not. During the reign of Antoninus Pius, a Greek called Pausanias wrote a *Description of Greece*, a sort of travel guide. In this he mentioned that Antoninus 'appropriated most of the territory of the Brigantes because they had begun a war, invading *Genunia*, which is subject to the Romans'. As it stands, this is nonsense. The Brigantes lay within the province, so we would not expect them to invade another part of the Roman dominions. Nor do we know where *Genunia* lay. Much ink has been spilt over trying to explain this enigmatic statement, but the best that we can do is to suggest that it may relate to a justification for the invasion of southern Scotland – the Romans always liked a 'just' war – but no more.

Officers and men

Roman sources do provide information on the people who took part in the invasion. The commander of the army was Quintus Lollius Urbicus. His home town was Cirta in Numidia, modern Constantine in Algeria. His first military service had been in legion XXII Primigenia based at Mainz in Upper Germany. After an appointment in Rome, he had served in Asia Minor, then as commander of legion X Gemina at Vienna. Service in Hadrian's Jewish war of the early 130s followed, in which he was decorated. Thence, he travelled across the empire to take up the governorship of Lower Germany. It was therefore a short step across the North Sea to Britain and the prestigious duty of extending the empire. In passing, we may note that Urbicus' career did not stop at this point: he went on to be proconsul of Asia and Prefect of the City of Rome. Urbicus was clearly a capable soldier. He had started life as the second son of a man who was not a senator, and rose, through his own abilities, to the most senior posts in the empire.

We also know the name of two of Urbicus' legionary commanders. Sisenna Rutilianus, son of a former governor of Britain, was legate of the Sixth Legion and Aulus Claudius Charax legate of the Second Legion. Charax appears to be a strange choice of officer. He was a Greek, a native of Pergamum in Asia Minor, and an historian. He was not a military man and had not previously served in any western province. There is, however, a link with the emperor. Antoninus had served as proconsul of Asia in 134–5 and while there is most likely to have met Charax, a leading citizen of the former capital of the Attalid kingdom: the two also shared an interest in history. Perhaps the emperor specifically chose Charax to share in the glory of this signal event.

The names of the other officers and men of the army are lost to us, but some, no doubt, will be those whose names were recorded on

Fig. 2.3 The priest officiating at the ceremony which was held before the invasion of Scotland was probably Aulus Claudius Charax, legate of the Second Legion Augusta.

the building stones of Hadrian's Wall for that frontier was still being constructed when it was abandoned in favour of the move north and some men will have had the dubious distinction of helping to build two Roman frontiers.

Britain was part of a vast empire. Its officials and soldiers criss-crossed that empire during their careers. Its administrators and soldiers obeyed the same laws, followed the same rules, celebrated the same religious ceremonies. 'Evidence by analogy' is therefore not just an acceptable but a necessary method of understanding the northern frontiers of Roman Britain. Our knowledge of the army of Britain may be based upon internal knowledge, but our information on its structure derives from empire-wide studies. We know that treaties governed the relationship between Rome and her northern neighbours in Britain, but not the details; contemporary treaties relating to other frontiers provide those details. The position of Britain within this empire, whose history and organisation are so well known to us, is of great value in helping us to understand its north-west frontier. Within this framework lie the internationally important Vindolanda writing-tablets. These not only illuminate life on the northern frontier of Britain – admittedly a generation or two before the building of the Antonine Wall – but their very similarity to other documents from elsewhere in the empire, and in particular the eastern provinces, allows us to use that evidence with confidence to shed further light on activities on our own frontier.

THE ANTONINE WALL

A major source of knowledge about the Antonine Wall is of course the structure itself. The Antonine Wall was marked on Matthew Paris' thirteenth-century map of Britain, and its location delineated on Timothy Pont's sixteenth-century map of Scotland. It was about the same time that historians started to write about the Wall. Some visited the remains themselves and left important records of the state of the Wall in their day. The most important of these was William Roy. A Scot, born in Carluke in Lanarkshire, Roy was commissioned

Fig. 2.4 The Antonine Wall is marked on Matthew Paris' map of Britain prepared in the thirteenth century.

Fig. 2.5 Timothy Pont plotted the Antonine Wall when he prepared his map of Scotland in the sixteenth century.

Fig. 2.6 In 1755 William Roy surveyed the Antonine Wall. This section of his map records the section over Croy Hill and Bar Hill.

to survey Scotland in the aftermath of the 1745/6 Jacobite Uprising. His interest in the Romans led him to survey the Antonine Wall in 1755. This was eventually published, posthumously, in his *The Military Antiquities of the Romans in Britain* (1793). His map

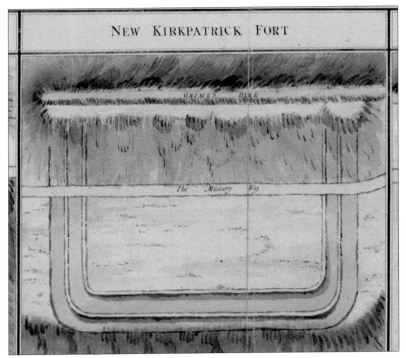

NEW KIRKPATRICK FORT

GRIMES DYKE

The Military Way

Fig. 2.7 The fort at New Kirkpatrick, now Bearsden, planned by William Roy.

remained the best record of the Wall until the Ordnance Survey maps were published in the 1860s and it is still a most valuable source of information. Its accuracy was demonstrated in 1973 when the fort at Bearsden (Roy's New Kirkpatrick) was excavated. Roy's measurements for the enclosure were found to be correct to within 1 foot (30 cm).

Since then, the Antonine Wall has been the subject of several mapping exercises by the Ordnance Survey and the records are managed by the Royal Commission on the Ancient and Historical Monuments of Scotland (RCAHMS) which adds new information as it becomes available.

The monument itself is not the only repository of information. Chance discoveries as well as artefacts from excavations are housed in museums in Scotland. Undoubtedly the most significant chance finds are those great items of sculpture, the distance slabs. Most

Fig. 2.8 The excavation of the granary at Rough Castle in 1903.

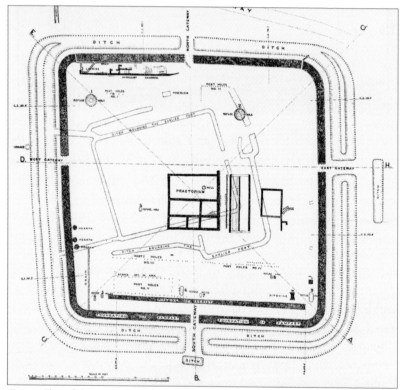

Fig. 2.9 Plan of the excavation of the fort at Bar Hill excavated in 1902–5. Not only was an enclosure discovered below the fort, but the timber barrack-blocks were identified and planned, particularly in the southern part of the fort.

found their way into the University of Glasgow and are now displayed in the Hunterian Museum. Their very magnificence has been a source of wonder and an inspiration to study the Wall.

Finally, today, much resides in records of many kinds. These include RCAHMS where all records of excavations are housed, libraries and studies which contain the published reports of survey, excavation and research. These demonstrate also the changing views and theories of the Wall, because much of our 'knowledge' is in fact the interpretation of scholars and that interpretation shifts, usually almost imperceptibly, but sometimes with a mighty lurch.

ARCHAEOLOGY

The era of modern excavation started on the Antonine Wall in the 1890s, as in much of Europe. The Glasgow Archaeological Society set out to discover if the Antonine Wall really was of turf and its members succeeded, probably beyond their wildest expectations. At the same time, the Society of Antiquaries of Scotland commenced a campaign of excavations on Roman military sites. It started at Birrens in 1895, moved on to Ardoch in 1896 and rose to a crescendo with the examination of Newstead from 1905 to 1910. Along the line of the Wall, the Society examined Camelon in 1900, Castlecary in 1902 and Rough Castle in 1903. The Glasgow Society continued to work in the west, at Bar Hill from 1902 to 1905, Balmuildy ten years later and Old Kilpatrick and Cadder between the two World Wars.

Most of these sites were excavated in order to learn more about the Antonine Wall, but others were examined as a result of development pressure arising from the location of the Antonine Wall within the industrial heartland of Scotland. Camelon was investigated in advance of the erection of iron works at Falkirk, Old Kilpatrick before – or rather at the same time as – the construction of houses, while gravel quarrying was the impetus for work at Cadder. This has continued to be the pattern.

1911 marked a significant year in the study of the Antonine Wall for it saw the publication of George Macdonald's *The Roman Wall*

Fig. 2.10 Sir George Macdonald in a trench at Mumrills in 1929.

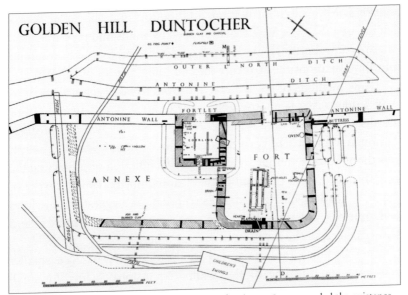

Fig. 2.11 Anne Robertson's excavation at Duntocher in 1948–51 revealed the existence of a fortlet next to the fort.

in Scotland. Here, in a monumental work, he brought together all the evidence for the Wall, the testimony of antiquarians and earlier visitors, the physical evidence of the remains themselves and the results of excavations and other studies of the frontier. It has only been surpassed by his own second edition published in 1934.

To prepare for both editions – and as a result of the thoughts arising from publishing them – Sir George, as he became, carried out excavations all along the Wall aimed at determining its location: this work is still one of the main bases of our mapping of the Antonine Wall. Macdonald also investigated several forts. These included Old Kilpatrick and Rough Castle where he was not content with the conclusions reached by earlier excavators. His work at Mumrills was something of a hybrid: World War I had prevented a research excavation and so the work which began in 1923 was a rescue excavation in advance of the construction of houses, most of which, as it happens, were not built.

Development pressures continued to be a major catalyst for excavation. The fort at Duntocher was examined in 1948–51, the annexe at Mumrills shortly after, and the fort and annexe at Bears-den in 1973–82. The Wall is also clipped by roads and pipe-trenches. All are now routinely excavated archaeologically with resulting information about the structure and building history of the Wall.

New methods of research have proved to be of major benefit to Wall studies. Aerial photography shortly after World War II led to the discovery of a new type of structure on the Wall: the fortlet. Although a fortlet had been discovered at Watling Lodge in 1894, it was thought to be unique, with the specific function of protecting the gate through which the road passed leading north. The discovery of the new fortlets changed that perception. A suggestion by John Gillam in 1975 that the few known sites were part of a more exten-sive series led to the location of several more.

Aerial photography also led to the discovery of even smaller enclosures on the line of the Wall. 'Expansions' – literally small expansions to the rear of the Wall – had long been known and inter-preted as beacon-platforms. The new discoveries were entirely different. They were small protected areas attached to the rear of the Wall. Only one has been excavated to date and it obstinately refused to reveal its function.

The third type of site discovered on the Wall through aerial archaeology is the temporary camp. Many temporary camps are now known along the line of the Antonine Wall, all located as a result of aerial photography over the last sixty years, and none visible today. Most are clearly labour camps occupied by the soldiers building the Wall. The fact that we appear to be able to relate the camps to the construction of the Wall, especially when combined with the evidence of the distance slabs and the differences in the structure of the Wall itself, is a unique element of the Antonine Wall.

The application of various new scientific tools has also helped us understand the Antonine Wall better. Natural sciences, such as botany, enable us to understand the vegetation history of the area and the diet of the soldiers as well as adding another dimension to our appreciation of the supply logistics of the frontier army. Geo-physical and magnetometer survey helps locate the Wall and its associated features.

Fig. 2.12 Pottery from the fort at Bearsden.

Archaeological research has continued. The promulgation of a new theory about the building of the Wall in 1975 brought archaeologists into the field to test it through application of the spade, and in that they were successful. Perseverance has finally led to the location of the long-lost fort in Falkirk. Sometimes wholly new and unexpected discoveries are made. One of these has been the location of pits on the berm, the space between the rampart and the ditch. These indicate that the Wall was more complex than hitherto understood and, perhaps, they help us understand its function better.

The artefacts – sculpture, coins, weapons, brooches, pottery, and so on – recovered during excavations have long been studied. The earliest reports from the 1890s contain accounts of these items. The pottery from the Antonine Wall is of particular interest as it is dated to such a short period, the relatively brief life of the Wall. However, pottery can provide other insights as well. It can, for example, inform us about supply and about the cooking methods of the soldiers and it has thus been realised that some vessels indicate that cooking was undertaken in an African style, with important implications for several different aspects of the occupation of the Antonine Wall, as we shall see.

SOURCES

The bid to add the Antonine Wall to the list of World Heritage Sites has been a great fillip to research and, as a result, will lead to greater knowledge and understanding of the Wall. The environmental history of the Wall area has been reviewed. Separate programmes of geophysical survey are seeking to locate the Military Way, the course of which is often uncertain, and civil settlements outside forts, about which we know relatively little. If necessary, excavations will be undertaken to clarify the line of the Wall and the Military Way. The method of mapping the Wall has been reviewed and the recording of information improved.

Today, we are in the ironic position of knowing more about the Antonine Wall than any of our predecessors yet at the same time appreciating that it has many more secrets to yield up. Some of these secrets will only be revealed through patient work in the study rather than in the field.

CHAPTER

III

THE ROMAN ARMY

Roman history is essentially the virtually unique story
of a nation trying to catch up with the situations produced
by the incredible success of its army.

JOHN MANN,
Britain and the Roman Empire (Aldershot 1996), 59

The Roman army was one of the most successful fighting forces that
the world has seen. For almost 800 years, from about 400 BC to AD
400, it rarely lost a war. It certainly lost battles: it was defeated by
Hannibal, by the Parthians, and in Germany, but in most cases it
recovered and either won or at least prevented any major erosion of
its power.

The Roman army in Britain was no different from its
counterparts elsewhere in the empire. The force which moved north
under Lollius Urbicus had seen near-continuous fighting for 100
years. Although Agricola's conquests in Scotland had been
abandoned within a decade of his invasion, warfare had not ceased.
During the reign of Trajan (98–117) a regiment was honoured for
meritorious conduct, perhaps as a result of fighting on the northern
frontier. When Hadrian came to the throne in 117, it was recorded
that the Britons could not be kept under control and a special coin
issue of 119 has been taken to mark victory in Britain. Rather later
in the reign, a special expeditionary force from the legions of Upper

Germany and Spain was sent to Britain. Cornelius Fronto remarked that the fighting in Britain under Hadrian was on such a serious scale that the losses merited comparison with those in the Jewish War of the early 130s. One casualty of these years was quite possibly a centurion buried at Vindolanda who had been killed in a war. Although the tombstone is not dated, the officer's regiment was based at the fort during the reigns of Trajan and Hadrian. It is not always clear whom the army fought. The main enemy faced by Agricola was the Caledonian people, while Severus campaigned against the Caledonians and Maeatae. Both lay north of the Antonine Wall. Pausanias mentions that the Brigantes began a war during the reign of Antoninus. The peoples of southern Scotland are otherwise not mentioned by name. In spite of such problems, it was clearly a battle-hardened force which marched north into Scotland.

THE PROVINCIAL ARMY

The Roman provincial army was divided into two main groups: the legions, composed of Roman citizens, and their support troops (literally auxiliaries) originally drawn from their allies. During the reign of Antoninus, there were three legions in Britain: the Second Augusta based at Caerleon-on-Usk, the Twentieth Valeria Victrix at Chester, and the Sixth Victrix at York, all some distance behind the frontier. The legions, each about 5,000 strong, were formed of highly-trained and heavily-armed infantry, with a small cavalry detachment. Each soldier wore a distinctive armour formed of metal strips to aid flexibility and was equipped with a sword, dagger, two spears and a rectangular shield; the cavalry wore mail shirts and fought with longer swords. Legions were organised into ten cohorts, each 480 strong, with the exception of the first which was formed of 800 men arranged in five double-strength centuries. Their length of service was twenty-five or twenty-six years: discharge appears to have taken place every other year.

The legionary commander was the *legatus legionis*, the legate of the legion, a senator, a member of the nobility holding his commission

Fig. 3.1 A Roman legionary of the early second century on the march.
Drawn by Peter Connolly.

Fig. 3.2 Standard-bearers on Trajan's Column.

directly from the emperor. Such a man was Aulus Claudius Charax, legate of the Second Legion. The second-in-command was the *tribunus laticlavius*, the tribune with a broad stripe, a man destined for the Senate. There were five other tribunes, all from the lower nobility. Each of these officers held his post for about three years during a career in the emperor's service which alternated military and civil positions. The third-in-command was the *praefectus castrorum*, the prefect of the camp; he was a professional soldier, having previously served as a centurion. The centurions, fifty-nine in total, had normally risen from the ranks and formed the backbone of the legion. Each commanded a century (*centuria*), nominally eighty strong. Upon them fell the day-to-day maintenance of discipline and efficiency. Each centurion had under him a second-in-command (the *optio*, so named because originally the centurion had exercised his option in choosing his deputy), a standard-bearer (*signifer*), and other junior officers. There was an elaborate system of junior officers and 'tradesmen' forming a highly-specialised administrative, clerical, surveying, engineering and building staff. The centurions – and other more senior officers – were allowed to marry, unlike the soldiers: the wife of a centurion of the Sixth Legion dedicated an altar at Westerwood on the Antonine Wall.

The legions formed the main building force on the Antonine Wall, though some work was undertaken by auxiliary units. It was mainly the auxiliary units which occupied the forts on the Wall, though legionaries are also attested on the frontier, apparently on garrison duty.

The auxiliaries differed from the legionaries in many ways. They were not recruited from Roman citizens, but from among the peoples of frontier provinces. The regiments on the Wall had originally been raised in provinces stretching from Spain to Syria, but once in Britain they usually recruited locally. One such soldier was Nectovelius who died at Mumrills on the Antonine Wall: he was a Brigantian by birth (see fig. 7.8). The army in Britain was augmented by soldiers from elsewhere. These were often Germans and Gauls, but might include men from other areas including the middle Danube (modern Austria and Hungary) and Africa.

Fig. 3.3 Auxiliary soldiers. The cavalryman stands to the left with his infantry colleague to the right. Drawn by Peter Connolly.

The auxiliaries were normally protected by mail shirts and armed with swords and spears and carried oval shields. There were six different types of regiments: cohorts of infantry and *alae* of cavalry, nominally either 1,000 (milliary) or 500 (quingenary) strong, with some cohorts (*cohortes equitatae*) containing a cavalry component of either 240 or 120 men in addition to the infantry core. The cohort was divided into ten or six centuries, each commanded by a centurion, an *ala* into twenty-four or sixteen troops (*turmae*), each commanded by a decurion. The 1,000-strong cohort was normally commanded by a tribune, the 500-strong cohorts and all cavalry regiments by a prefect. Tribunes and prefects were members of the lower nobility, and normally held their posts for about three years. The centurions and decurions, as in the legions, had risen from the ranks and were supported by junior officers and specialist staff. The length of service was twenty-five years, apart from the centurions and decurions who appear to have had no formal retirement age.

Auxiliary soldiers received Roman citizenship on retirement, and it seems probable that the number of citizens in such regiments grew as sons of citizen soldiers joined their fathers' units. On retirement, an auxiliary soldier could apply for a copy of the document which recorded that he had been awarded Roman citizenship: these are known as diplomas. While the purpose of the diploma was to detail the privileges given to the recipient, they have great advantages for us in that they are made of bronze and they list all the regiments who discharged soldiers at the same time. Several diplomas are known from Britain, ranging in date from 98 to 178. Five are known from the reign of Antoninus. Unfortunately, these are so fragmentary that two provide no information on units and two others each only mention a single unit. The fifth diploma, dating to 146, found at Chesters in the nineteenth century, lists three cavalry regiments and eleven cohorts. Two of these cohorts are known to have been based on the Antonine Wall as well as the two cohorts recorded on the other two diplomas. The Chesters' diploma is one of two relating to the British army known to have been issued in 146.

The diplomas of the reigns of Antoninus and Marcus Aurelius list twelve cavalry regiments and forty-four infantry regiments in Britain. Together with the legions the theoretical strength of the army would be nearly 50,000 troops, accepting our best guess for unit size. The very few reports which survive, however, indicate that units were often below strength, in one case by as much as 25 per cent. This would reduce the size of the provincial army to 37,500–40,000 men.

There were two other groups within the provincial army. The British fleet (*classis Britannica*) was the naval branch of the empire's military forces. Based in the English Channel, its forces were employed to protect the empire's coasts from hostile action. There is no clear evidence that the fleet was involved in supply: this was normally carried out by civilian contractors. Neither is it recorded operating in Scotland at this time. The second group was a collection of units known as *numeri*. They are first attested on Hadrian's Wall about 200 but none is known in Scotland.

The Roman army was a well-trained, highly disciplined fighting machine, more than a match for any force which could be put into

UNIT	NUMBER IN BRITAIN	STRENGTH OF EACH	TOTAL STRENGTH
legions	3	5,120	15,360
1,000-strong cavalry regiment	1	768	768
500-strong cavalry regiments	11	512	5,632
1,000-strong mixed infantry and cavalry units	5	1,056	5,280
1,000-strong infantry units	2	800	1,600
500-strong mixed infantry and cavalry units	18	608	10,944
500-strong infantry units	19	480	9,120
GRAND TOTAL			48,704

Table 3 Strength of the army of Britain during the reign of Antoninus

the field against it. Potential recruits had to meet basic qualifications: they had to be of appropriate legal status, that is free born, and had to pass a medical examination as well as meet the height qualification, probably 1.75 m (5 feet 8–10 inches). The recruit was normally aged between eighteen and twenty-one years of age. If accepted, each recruit would receive basic training in arms and weapons, drill and manoeuvres, running and jumping, military discipline and camp building. Training did not then cease, but continued throughout the soldier's career. Such training included marching at military and rapid paces, swimming, vaulting over wooden horses, tree-felling and cross-country marches of 32 km (20 miles) three times a month. Parade grounds and perhaps amphitheatres were provided for training purposes. Special exercises were undertaken and some of these are described for us by Roman authors: the bronze face masks found at Newstead would have been worn on such occasions.

One important aspect of training was learning how to construct a temporary camp while on the march and where to pitch the tents within it. Each night while on campaign such a camp was constructed. In 82 the Ninth Legion was attacked at night: its camp defences prevented it from being overwhelmed. The lack of a properly fortified camp, for example, contributed to the defeat of the British army at the hands of the Zulus at Isandhlwana in 1879. It was not just a battle-hardened force which marched into Scotland, but a well-trained army too.

CHAPTER IV

THE INVASION
OF SCOTLAND

IMPERATOR II
(Conqueror for the second time)

Roman Imperial Coinage, 745

The Roman army which crossed the Cheviots was not entering unknown territory. By this time, the Romans had been in Britain for nearly one hundred years. Indeed, the two invasions by Julius Caesar had occurred nearly 200 years prior to Urbicus' expedition. The Romans had considerable knowledge of the geography of north Britain. They knew that Britain was an island, and that there were various archipelagos off its northern and western coasts. Even before the first invasions of Scotland by Agricola in the late 70s, Roman geographers had recorded that there were thirty Orkney islands (there are actually about sixty, but only twenty-nine inhabited islands in 1900) and seven islands in Shetland, while the existence of the Hebrides was also known. Several writers mentioned Caledonia and the Caledonian Forest, which, it would appear, had already become a phrase indicative of the edge of the world.

THE INVASION OF BRITAIN

The invasion of Britain by Claudius in 43 led to the establishment of a province in the area that now forms southern and eastern England together with the Midlands. Its northern frontier was secured through a treaty with the Brigantes who occupied most of northern England. The western frontier faced Wales and was the scene of near continuous warfare for thirty years. The death of Nero in 68 and the accession of Vespasian radically changed the situation. The new emperor had first-hand experience of Britain having served in the island during the invasion. He would appear to have decided on a new forward policy for Britain and during the 70s sent successively three experienced governors to command his armies. The first task was the restoration of order on the northern frontier. Rome's client queen, Cartimandua, had been expelled from her kingdom and Petillius Cerialis brought the state within the empire. His successor, Julius Frontinus, dealt with Wales. He was followed by Julius Agricola. Of the three, he is the best known today for the biography written by his historian son-in-law, Tacitus, has survived. Agricola was unusual in that all his military experience had been gained within Britain.

Agricola's actions led to a major extension of the province. He served in Britain for seven seasons, quelling a revolt by the Ordovices of north Wales, invading and conquering southern Scotland and establishing a series of garrison posts across the Forth–Clyde isthmus and then, after a break of two years, invading northern Scotland and defeating the Caledonians at the Battle of Mons Graupius in late 83. His unknown successor set about controlling the new territory. A new legionary fortress was built on the River Tay and a screen of auxiliary forts laid down along the edge of the Highlands. They may have been intended as the north limit of the empire or as the springboards for an invasion of the Highlands. We will never know because Roman defeats on the lower Danube led to a withdrawal of troops from Britain – perhaps a quarter of the army – and the abandonment of the newly gained territories. The army withdrew to a line not far different from the modern Anglo-Scottish border. By about 100 the most northerly troops appear to have been based along the Tyne–Solway isthmus, the narrowest point in northern England.

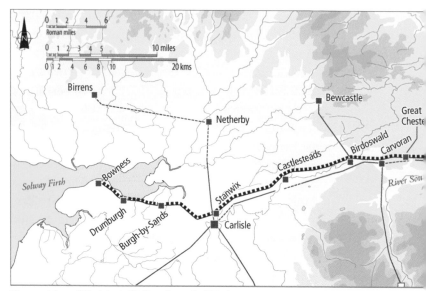

Fig. 4.1 Map of Hadrian's Wall at the end of Hadrian's reign.

HADRIAN'S WALL

It was here, in 122, that the emperor Hadrian decided to build the Wall which now bears his name. He retained the existing line of forts across the isthmus, and built his Wall a short distance to the north, utilising the landform most effectively. From Newcastle westwards for about 50 km (30 miles), the Wall ran along a ridge to the north of the Tyne valley. Through its central sector it used the crags as a convenient line. On descending from the crags, it resumed a position on the north side of the river, in this case the Irthing which flows into the Eden just east of Carlisle. From Carlisle to Bowness, the most westerly 56 km (34 miles) of the Wall lie on the south edge of the Solway estuary.

Hadrian's Wall was planned to be a stone wall for its easterly 80 km (50 miles) with the western 50 km (30 miles) built of turf (though it was later converted to stone). The stone wall was to be 10 Roman feet (2.92 m) wide and probably 15 Roman feet (4.3 m) high; the turf wall was 20 Roman feet (5.84 m) wide and perhaps a little less tall than the stone sector. In front lay a ditch, except where the

Fig. 4.2 Hadrian's Wall at Cuddy's Crag looking east.

crags or the river or sea made this superfluous. At every mile there
was a gate surmounted by a tower and protected by a small enclosure, normally containing a barrack-block for the soldiers; this we
term a milecastle. Between each pair of milecastles lay two towers
(today called turrets). This sequence of towers provided elevated

observation platforms at every one-third of a mile. Although most reconstruction drawings place a wall-walk along the top of the Wall, there is no firm evidence for this and the very density of the towers may have rendered it unnecessary.

The Wall was constructed by soldiers of the three legions of Britain. The original intention appears to have been to divide the Wall up into 5-mile lengths, each to be built by one legion. From the first season, this plan seems to have gone awry.

Before the original scheme was completed, it was radically altered in two ways. Firstly, forts were added to the line of the Wall. Many were actually built astride the Wall with three of their four main gates to the north of the barrier. It seems probable that this was in reaction to the erection of a great barrier which restricted free movement of the army, the Wall itself. The army now sought to provide its soldiers with as much mobility as possible. Secondly, a great earthwork, known since the time of the Venerable Bede over 1,000 years ago as the Vallum, was constructed behind the Wall. It should probably be seen as the Roman equivalent of barbed wire, making a definitive statement: this is the edge of military territory. The effect of the Vallum was to reduce the number of crossing points as now they were only found at forts, where causeways protected by gates were provided. Thus movement in the frontier zone was considerably restricted. In the first plan, it would have been possible to cross the Wall at any one of eighty milecastles. It was now allowed only at the thirteen or fourteen forts and, presumably, the gates on the roads north. The reason for this major change is not clear. Perhaps the army wished to bring movement under the more immediate eye of the senior officers in the forts; possibly it resulted from disturbance within the province or on the frontier – a serious war is known to have taken place within Britain, which may be dated to this time.

Other changes to the Wall probably resulted from the increasing complexity of the frontier. The stone wall was narrowed from 10 Roman feet (2.92 m) to 8 Roman feet (2.34 m) or less, while the standard of craftsmanship declined dramatically. However, even so, Hadrian's Wall was still being modified when its initiator died.

As we have seen, one immediate decision of Hadrian's successor was to abandon his frontier. Although, the Wall was presumably not decommissioned immediately, archaeological investigation of the structures along the Wall has indicated that milecastles and turrets were abandoned. Movement across the frontier line was now allowed through the removal of milecastle gates and the slighting of the Vallum. The order was clearly to tip earth from each mound of the Vallum into its ditch at a regular spacing of 41 m (45 yards). This operation was not completed, however, as there are many stretches visible today where the work was not undertaken.

The invasion of Scotland

Any military expedition would normally gather intelligence before it marched out. We have seen that the Romans had considerable geographical knowledge of Britain. No map, in the modern sense, has survived from antiquity, but we have road lists of distances and other information in tabulated form.

Both Caesar and Tacitus record the army seeking information from merchants and travellers as well as refugees. Tacitus states that the routes to Ireland and its harbours were known to the Romans of the late first century through trade and merchants. Reconnaissance parties might be sent out: Caesar despatched Volusenus in a ship to reconnoitre potential landing places on the north side of the Channel before he sailed with the main army in 55 BC. On the march, mounted scouts would be continually surveying the country ahead. Prisoners, deserters and local people would all be pressed into service during the campaign. To aid the process, the army employed interpreters and mappers.

We have no idea how the army moved into Scotland. It presumably followed normal procedure and constructed marching camps to protect itself each evening when it stopped. Although some camps on the main routes north — the lines of the modern A68 and M6/M74 which themselves adopt the route of their Roman predecessors – are considered to date to this time, they do not form

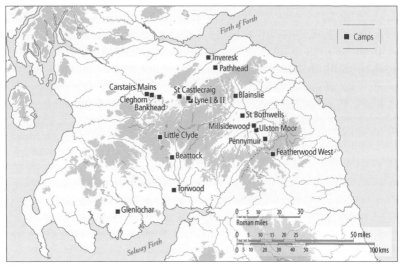

Fig. 4.3 Camps in Scotland considered to date to the Antonine period.

a coherent pattern. Nor has any potential marching camp of this period had its date confirmed through excavation, while those which are considered to date to this time are significantly smaller than those camps which have been allocated to the Severan campaigns of the early third century. This, however, may merely indicate that the army was operating in smaller groups. As the area through which the army marched had been conquered sixty years before and, we may believe, been under Roman surveillance for the previous fifty years, the march may be seen as a walk-over rather than a serious military operation.

THE ENEMY

Even if the enemy did fight, we know little of their fighting tactics. Tacitus records that in the first century the Caledonians still used chariots, but fought on foot. Cassius Dio and Herodian mention chariots in the early third century when discussing the Caledonians and Maeatae, with the foot soldiers armed with shields, spears, swords and daggers. Equally interestingly, the Caledonians used hit-

Fig. 4.4 The scene to the left of the Bridgeness distance slab shows a Roman cavalryman riding down a group of four barbarians – or perhaps the scene depicts the various stages in the death of a single enemy.

and-run tactics, the best approach to such a well-disciplined and well-armed force such as the Roman army. Even so, none of the guerrilla wars waged in Britain against the Romans was successful.

There is one final but very valuable account to note. One of the Vindolanda writing tablets dating to about 100 states that '... the Britons are unprotected by armour (?). There are very many cavalry. The cavalry do not use swords nor do the wretched Britons mount in order to throw javelins.' The status of this document is not known, nor are the Britons described within it otherwise identified: are they enemies, or new recruits to the army?

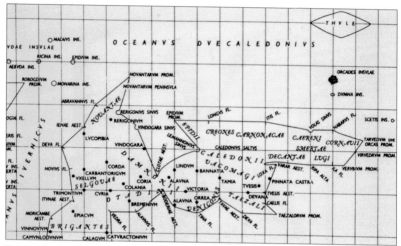

Fig. 4.5 Ptolemy's map of north Britain.

Although we know the names of the tribes living in this area –
through the *Geography* of the contemporary Ptolemy of Alexandria
– we know almost nothing of their reaction to Rome. The Votadini
occupied modern Northumbria, the eastern Border lands and
Lothian. To the south-west, in Dumfries and Galloway, lay the
Novantae, while in between were the Selgovae, centred on
Annandale and Nithsdale. In Ayrshire and the Glasgow area were the
Dumnonii. Although Ptolemy records the location of these tribes,
there is some reason to doubt the accuracy of his information.
Gathering information at a distance, and using different sources, he
may have added some names to the wrong list and even omitted one
or more tribal names.

Archaeologists have sought to ascribe affiliations to these tribes
on the basis of the distribution of Roman forts and artefacts. Thus,
the Votadini are regarded as pro-Roman because of the discovery of
many Roman objects at Traprain Law which we believe was their
capital. The Selgovae, on the other hand, are seen as anti-Roman
because of the density of Roman forts within their territory.
However, forts were located for several reasons including proximity
to lines of communication and good farmland. The forts in
Annandale and Nithsdale are located beside roads running up to the

Fig. 4.6 A striking depiction of a soldier wielding an axe on Trajan's Column.

frontier, with many close to the good farmlands of the valleys. A further twist is that often generals preferred to place their troops in friendly territory, knowing that they could move quickly to quell disturbances in the territory of neighbouring tribes if necessary. Unfortunately, therefore, the location of Roman forts does not help us determine the political views of the tribes of southern Scotland during the second century.

While, according to Ptolemy, the land between the Tyne–Solway isthmus and the Highlands was divided amongst several tribes, all these people lived in much the same manner. Clearance of the natural woodland of north Britain had been underway for centuries. About two or three centuries before the arrival of the Romans, however, there was an increase in activity and within a generation most of the remaining woodland was removed so that the Roman army would have crossed a landscape probably bearing less woodland than today. This landscape would have been occupied by farms, and divided into fields between lanes and tracks. The houses were usually built of wood and round in shape, though still spacious, with the living area assigned to different uses. Sometimes the farm and its attendant yard were defined by a bank and ditch. Cattle, sheep and pig were all raised, while crops included wheat, barley, oats and rye. We know little of the material culture of these people. Weapons and ornaments are rarely found, though those that are discovered are of high quality. Little pottery appears to have been used and this is the more surprising in view of the lack of evidence for trees from which wooden vessels could be made.

The army on the march

As the army was moving through territory under surveillance for many years, and through states possibly even in treaty relationship with Rome and certainly about to become part of the Roman empire, it may be that it did not follow the procedures of foraging while on campaign, but left the farms of southern Scotland unmolested and relied upon its own supplies. The army would normally carry

Fig. 4.7 Carts drawn by mules and oxen on Trajan's Column.

Fig. 4.8 The Ingliston milestone on the Roman road leading north to the Antonine Wall probably dates to 140–4 and indicates that the communications network was being prepared for the new occupation of Scotland.

supplies to last seven days. It is highly unlikely that the soldiers would carry much themselves. Mules, mule- and ox-drawn carts would bear most of the burdens – not just food, but cooking implements, tents, and all the other paraphernalia required on campaign. Seven days would be sufficient time for the army to march from Hadrian's Wall to the line chosen for the new frontier. The most efficient way to bring up new supplies was by sea.

The single most remarkable aspect of the Roman invasion of Scotland in 140 is that it must have been very straightforward. There is no evidence that the peoples of southern Scotland ever gave the army any trouble, though this may simply reflect our poor sources. The area brought into the empire was restricted in extent: the army could easily have mopped up any dissent within a matter of months. What did it do with the rest of the time between its rebuilding at Corbridge in 139 and the victory celebrated in 142?

REWARDS AND DECORATIONS

At the end of the campaign, we may presume that decorations were handed out. During the reign of Antoninus, the soldiers of the First Baetasian Cohort were awarded Roman citizenship and the regiment acknowledged that honour in its title. It seems probable that it was at this time that the First Spanish Cohort was granted the honour of adding the emperor's family name, *Aelia*, to its titles.

The successful military operation was also recorded in a rather different way. Three kilometres (2 miles) north of the Antonine Wall, beside the River Carron, stood Arthur's O'on (oven), a circular domed structure of dressed stones set in mortar (see fig. 4.10), until its destruction in 1743. This structure has been interpreted as a Roman temple, possibly dedicated to the goddess Victory. The discovery of a brass finger inside the structure not long before its destruction suggests the former existence of a cult statue. The construction of victory monuments by the Romans is not unknown and this is likely to have been the purpose of Arthur's O'on.

The Romans may have drafted some of the defeated tribesmen

Fig. 4.9 An inscription recording a unit of Britons on the German frontier.

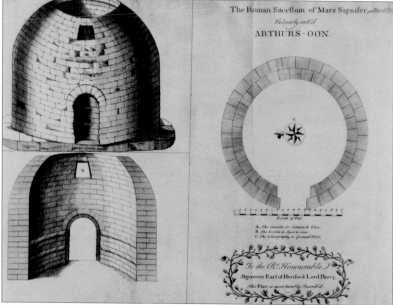

Fig. 4.10 Arthur's O'on.

into their army. Nearly twenty auxiliary units of Britons – both cavalry and infantry – are recorded elsewhere in the empire and at least seven lower grade units known as *numeri* appear on the Upper German frontier. Some of the auxiliary units were recruited before the first invasion of Scotland under Agricola; others bear titles indicating that they were raised, or at least honoured, under the Flavians (Vespasian, Titus and Domitian), in the brief reign of Nerva from 96 to 98, or under Trajan and Hadrian and their immediate successors. Although the *numeri* in Germany are not attested until the middle years of the second century, several occupy forts of a type first constructed rather earlier. It may be that some were recruited following the Agricolan advance, though the process may have been repeated in the 140s.

There were also new provincials to organise. At some stage there would have to be a census, for now they would have to pay taxes to Rome. Perhaps new treaties had to be negotiated with the states beyond the frontier. But for the army, the main task was the construction of a new frontier.

CHAPTER V

THE ANTONINE WALL

The wall of Antoninus, like other works of the same
sort, consists of three parts; a large ditch, a rampart, with
its parapet behind it, and a military way behind both.

W. ROY,
The Military Antiquities of the Romans in Britain
(London 1793), 156

The first task of the army would have been to choose a line for the Wall and then survey its position in detail. For this purpose the legions contained surveyors (*mensores*). They would have been in the advance guard, as they were when the army was on the march.

The line chosen was good and commands respect even today. The east end was to be at modern Bridgeness at the eastern end of the modern town of Bo'ness. It is not entirely clear why this particular location was chosen, though it is the point where the coastline turns sharply in a south-easterly direction. From here, westwards for about 8 km (5 miles) it lies on top of the steep slope overlooking the Firth of Forth: this bank was a raised beach of some antiquity. For a short distance, the country is broken by streams cutting through, and then the Wall takes a line along the edge of the Central Valley of Scotland formed by the Rivers Carron and Kelvin. The Wall lies on the forward slope on the south side of the valley in a superb position for observation. The Central Valley would also

Fig. 5.1 The Kelvin Valley looking west with the Campsie Fells to the right.

have been much boggier than today, aiding the Roman position.

About 13 km (8 miles) from the western end of the Wall it is crossed by the River Kelvin and for the next 6.5 km (4 miles) it follows a more irregular route, moving from one high point to another before adopting a straighter course to Old Kilpatrick. We presume that the Wall stretched far enough west to control most of the fording points over the River Clyde. To the best of our knowledge, only one major ford, at Bowling, lay beyond the Wall.

In some significant ways, the landforms were very different 2,000 years ago. Much land has been reclaimed from the sea in the Firth of Forth so that the area on which modern Grangemouth is constructed would have been underwater. The sea level was also slightly higher than today. Thus water would have lapped the foot of the slope on which the Wall sits from Bo'ness to Inveravon and possibly lay immediately in front of the fort at Inveravon. However, mudflats would have extended well out into the estuary providing rather a different impression of the Roman position at low tide. At

Fig. 5.2 The Antonine Wall crossing Croy Hill looking west.

Fig. 5.3 The straight line of the German frontier is still a significant feature in the landscape of today.

the west end, the River Clyde was much shallower than today, also with wide mudflats exposed at low tide, while water in the main channel was probably a metre less deep than it was before modern dredging.

The Antonine Wall took a more sinuous course than its predecessor, Hadrian's Wall. Both, however, used the landscape to good effect. They took advantage of ridges, cliffs, rivers and hills to create, wherever possible, an advantageous line. The German frontier, also constructed during the reign of Antoninus, was entirely different. One stretch followed a straight line for a distance of 80 km (50 miles), in the process riding up and down many river valleys which crossed its line: it simply ignored all natural features.

The Antonine Wall would have cut across a well-farmed landscape. Within this countryside, there was no 'free' land on which to place the Wall. Indeed, its construction would have created a brand-new line across the landscape, as railways were to do in the nineteenth century and motorways in the twentieth. Like modern farmers, we might expect that their predecessors were recompensed for their losses. The Roman empire followed the rule of law and its citizens had a healthy respect for property rights: when the Emperor Domitian created a new frontier in Germany in 83, he ordered that compensation be paid for the loss of crops.

The history of the use of the landscape before the arrival of the Romans affected what was available to them in the form of building materials. As we will see, there was plenty of grassland to lift for turves in fields of pasture grazed by cattle and sheep. By the time the Wall builders arrived, much of the earlier oak woodland had been cut down and replaced by light scrubland containing alder, ash, birch, hazel, rowan and willow. Yet there was probably still enough woodland within about a 3-km (2-mile) radius of each fort to meet the timber requirements.

Sixty years before the building of the Antonine Wall, Agricola had placed a line of garrison posts across the Forth–Clyde isthmus. The locations of three are known: Camelon on the western outskirts of Falkirk, Mollins west of Cumbernauld and Barochan near Bishopton on the south side of the Clyde. None of these lay on the line of the Wall. Some forts on the Wall have yielded artefacts of first-century date – Mumrills, Castlecary and Cadder – but no structural evidence. It would appear that the second-century surveyors ignored the past and chose the most effective line for the Wall for their purposes.

THE BUILDERS

While the surveying was underway, the force gathered to build the Wall would no doubt have been making its preparations. Inscriptions, now known as distance slabs, from the structure itself demonstrate that it was constructed by soldiers from the three legions of the province: legions II Augusta, VI Victrix and XX Valeria Victrix. The first was present in full strength, but the other two only sent detachments. It is difficult therefore to know how many men were provided. Certainly not even the whole of the Second Legion would have been present as many men would have remained at base,

Fig. 5.4 The Bridgeness distance slab is the largest to have been found on the Wall.

while others may have been on duty elsewhere: we might guess that 3,000–4,000 of its soldiers moved up to the Wall. The other groups were smaller, each perhaps no more than 2,000 strong, that is each consisted of four cohorts. The total legionary strength may have been no more than 8,000 men.

The legions were supported by auxiliary units, who are recorded building forts. As building inscriptions of both legionaries and auxiliaries survive at various forts, a straightforward division of labour may not be the simplest solution. Legionaries are attested building at Castlecary and Bar Hill, while Rough Castle, Castlecary and Bar Hill have each furnished an inscription recording building work by an auxiliary unit.

These soldiers built the Wall themselves. Each legion included surveyors, architect-engineers, masons, carpenters, even glaziers. These men cut the stones themselves, lifted the turves, put both into place, dug the ditches, cut timber: there is no evidence that civilians

were involved in this operation. Wherever possible, these materials would have been gathered from close to the Wall.

The distance slabs show that the whole length of the Wall was broken up into blocks of work, each assigned to a legion. The western 6 km (4 miles) were measured independently, but the rest of the Wall was divided into blocks of varying length: 4⅔, 3⅔ and 3 Roman miles long. These distances are very particular: 4,652, 3,660.8 and 3,666.5 paces. This indicates a very detailed specification for the building work. Mark Hassall has observed that adding the 3,660.8 paces and the 3,000 paces recorded as being built by the Twentieth Legion in the central sector of the Wall furnishes a total of 6,660.8 paces, that is 6.6608 Roman miles, almost exactly a third of 20 miles, which is half the length of the Wall – with the forts excluded. The six lengths at the west end of the Wall, all measured in feet, total 2 miles, leaving the eastern 14 miles to be divided into three lengths, each of about 4,666.6 paces, close to the distance recorded on the Bridgeness distance slab, 4,652 paces.

There is an attractive symmetry to these figures, which also

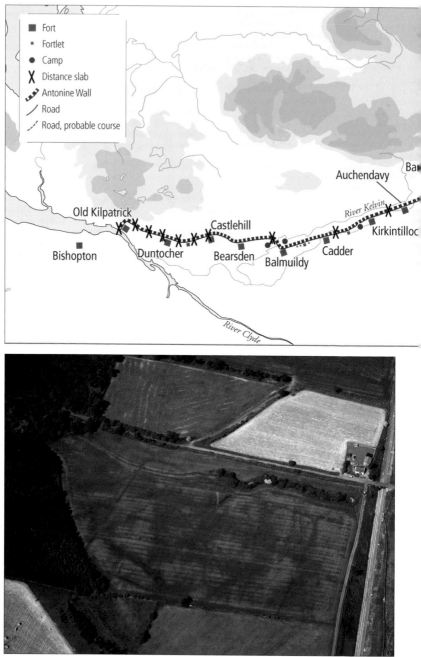

Fort
Fortlet
Camp
Distance slab
Antonine Wall
Road
Road, probable course

Auchendavy

Old Kilpatrick

River Kelvin

Castlehill

Kirkintilloc

Bishopton

Duntocher

Bearsden

Balmuildy

Cadder

River Clyde

Fig. 5.5 The labour camp at Tamfourhill.

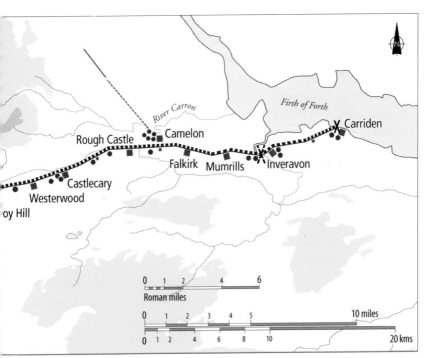

Fig. 5.6 The locations of the known distance slabs and labour camps along the Antonine Wall.

relate to the precise measurements of the distance slabs. Other theories are possible, however. The 4,652 paces of the Bridgeness distance slab is about one-ninth of the length of the Wall, leading to the possibility that the original plan was to divide the Wall into three three-legion lengths. If this was the case, the original plan was soon disrupted. Nor does this theory explain the detailed measurements of the central sector. In short, there is much to be said for the Hassall proposition.

It was normal for soldiers on building duty to be protected while they slept by the construction of a temporary camp, a labour camp. Twenty camps are known along the line of the Wall. A group at Camelon clearly relates to armies on the march north, but it may be presumed that most, if not all, of the rest were used by the soldiers building the Wall. Only two have produced dating evidence, Little Kerse and Dullatur, in both cases pottery of mid-second-century date.

It is typical of the haphazard nature of the evidence that while most of the distance slabs have been found in the western half of the Wall, the best evidence for the labour camps is from the east. Most of the camps range in size from 2 to 2.5 ha (5 to 6 acres) in size. At each end of the eastern 4¾ miles of the Wall are two labour camps. The four camps between them could have held a complete legion, depending on whether supplies were retained within the camps. At the eastern end of the next length to the west are also two camps. It would appear that the soldiers worked from each end towards the middle as they built the Wall, but how they divided the work between them is another matter. Was there a rampart gang and a ditch gang? Near two forts, Castlecary and Balmuildy, camps have been recorded, two at the former site. The existence of these large camps may indicate that the fort builders were housed separately, though the ditch of one of the camps at Castlecary butted against the rear face of the Wall, demonstrating that it was later, so the situation is not clear.

It would be wrong to give the impression that the camps can be explained and related to the building programme. At Dullatur, the camp was reoccupied, while the camp at Castlecary was clearly constructed after the Wall, as we have seen. At present we do not understand these anomalies, though it is possible that they relate to the long building history of the Wall.

Excavation has revealed a small enclosure beneath each of the forts at Croy Hill and Bar Hill (see fig. 2.9); both enclosures appear to have been of a temporary nature. They are much smaller than normal temporary camps, containing a mere 0.4 ha (about an acre) and 0.2 ha (0.5 acres) respectively, each with an annexe to the side. A road was noted within the enclosure on Croy Hill and foundations for a building at Bar Hill. A third, even smaller enclosure lay east of the fort at Mumrills. It was protected by a single ditch and earthen rampart, broken by an entrance to the north. Some post-holes were found in the interior, but no pattern could be discerned. A single sherd of Antonine pottery found in the ditch indicated the date. It is possible that all relate to the surveying phase of the Wall rather than the subsequent building activity.

Fig. 5.7 This distance slab is from Hutcheson Hill.

THE DISTANCE SLABS

The distance slabs form the most important collection of Roman military sculpture on any Roman frontier. Their primary purpose was to record how much of the Wall each legion had constructed. One stone was placed at each end of every legionary length, not just on the south face but apparently on the north side as well. Such records are known on Hadrian's Wall, but there the stones are much simpler and they do not record any distances. The Antonine Wall stones, in contrast, are all much more ornately carved. Even the simplest is quite distinct from the Hadrianic records on the southern frontier.

There is one distance slab with no ornamentation. Otherwise the more straightforward stones are simply decorated. Two legions adorned their stones with their symbols: a boar for the Twentieth and a capricorn and a pegasus for the Second. Several stones commemorate the victorious Roman army, either with a scene showing a Roman soldier riding down barbarians, or through the depiction of a captured enemy. The goddess Victory appears on four stones, on two of which she is awarding a laurel wreath to the legion. On one stone, she sits before her temple holding a large laurel wreath. Strangely, two stones are decorated with what appear to be cupids.

Two stones in particular stand out. The Bridgeness distance slab found at the east end of the Wall in 1868 bears two scenes (see fig. 5.4). The right-hand panel shows the ceremony held before the start of fighting. A priest, almost certainly Aulus Claudius Charax commander of the legion, offers a sacrifice to the gods of a bull, sheep and pig. The placing of this stone at the eastern end of the Wall is perhaps further evidence that the building of the frontier started from this end. In the left-hand scene a Roman cavalryman rides down a group of four opponents, or, more probably, the scene shows one enemy at various stages of defeat, culminating in decapitation.

The other distance slab was found a hundred years later in 1969 at Hutcheson Hill towards the west end of the Wall (see fig. 5.7). In the central panel, the goddess Victory is placing a laurel wreath in the beak of the eagle of the Twentieth Legion, watched from each side by a kneeling captured enemy.

Taken as a group, these are triumphalist records of conflict and conquest celebrating the Roman army's victory over an enemy who is always shown naked, dejected, bound or mutilated. They are statements of imperial power: there is no doubt who won. Taken as a group, they also tell the story of the invasion, from the preceding ceremonial sacrifice to the gods, through the fighting to the Roman victory. The appropriate Roman goddess, Victory, rewards the Romans, while the defeated enemy watch in submissive pose.

In some ways, the distance slabs might be seen as naïve pieces of work. The legionary sculptors, however, were clearly capable craftsmen and produced work which has vitality as well as a certain originality while still drawing on well-known stereotypes. Their vitality would have been enhanced by paint. Traces of red paint, for example, have been found on one stone.

The backs of most slabs reveal that they were once attached in some way to the Antonine Wall. These stones exhibit small cramp-holes on their top and side edges. It would appear, therefore, that they were set and secured within a frame. Sandstone blocks were found with the Bridgeness distance slab and may have formed part of its base. At Tollpark, an additional length of stone foundation behind the Wall could relate to a later repair to the rampart, but its use as a platform for one or two distance slabs cannot be totally rejected.

The distance slabs provide one final piece of useful information, what the army called the Antonine Wall: the *vallum*. The work that they undertook, according to the inscriptions, was the *opus valli*, the work of building a rampart.

One final question remains: why were the distance slabs so ornate? We cannot know the answer to this. The building of the much more solid Hadrian's Wall was marked by far simpler stones. It has been suggested that the distance slabs offered a counterbalance to the slighter built northern frontier. No such ornate inscriptions occur on that stretch of the German frontier built under Antoninus Pius; indeed, hardly any building inscriptions are known on that frontier. Perhaps, therefore, we come back to the reason for the reconquest of southern Scotland. If its purpose was specifically to provide the new emperor with military prestige, the distance slabs certainly clearly stated that a Roman victory had been won, the enemy vanquished, the empire extended – Antoninus acquired the honour of being a *propagator imperii* in the traditional manner – and that the gods smiled on the Roman empire – and its emperor.

THE ANTONINE WALL

There were three essential linear elements to the Wall: the rampart, the ditch, with the earth from it tipped out to the north to create an outer or upcast mound, in military terms a glacis. Behind the Wall ran a fourth feature, the Military Way.

The rampart was erected on a stone base, probably intended to

Fig. 5.8 The Antonine Wall at Rough Castle, Bonnybridge, looking east. The turf rampart survives as a low mound with the ditch to the left.

be 15 Roman feet (4.44 m) wide. Rough stones, often rounded cobbles from streams and rivers, were used to form the base, which was bounded by dressed kerbs. Occasionally, junctions between two gangs of builders have been noted in the base. Culverts crossed the stone base, so as to prevent water from ponding up on one side of the Wall. These may have occurred at regular intervals: there were three relatively close together at Bantaskin. If so, this was a lesson learnt from Hadrian's Wall where regular culverts were not provided in the original scheme. These culverts caused some problems on the downhill side for water debouching from them undermined the Wall and led to a requirement for repairs in these areas.

The question may be asked, why the Antonine rampart was placed on a stone base. Hadrian's turf wall was erected on a turf platform, and, at 20 Roman feet (6 m), it was wider. A stone base would have provided greater stability and, albeit narrower, would presumably have allowed the rampart to have been built to the same height. A stone base may also have allowed for better drainage, not just at the bottom of the rampart, but through the base.

There is evidence that the original intention may have been to

Fig. 5.9 The stone base of the Antonine Wall in New Kilpatrick Cemetery, Bearsden.

Fig. 5.10 A section cut through the Antonine Wall in 1959. The excavation was undertaken by Professor Anne Robertson in advance of a pipeline. The turves are visible, and the stone base on which they sat.

construct the rampart in stone rather than turf. Two of the primary forts have stone walls, and one, Balmuildy, has stone wing walls as if the builders were expecting to link their fort to a stone wall (see fig. 5.15). If this was the original intention, it was soon abandoned.

A fourth-century Roman military manual states that the regulation size for turves was 18 by 12 by 6 inches (45 by 30 by 15 cm). That may have been the regulation size, but relatively few turves on the Wall respond closely to it! Turves of this size are difficult to carry. If held in front in the hands, they can easily fold together and fall to the ground. Soldiers therefore carried them on their shoulders, as depicted on Trajan's Column (see fig. 6.15). A short length of rope served to secure the turf while being carried.

Although it is commonly stated that the Antonine Wall was built of turf, a considerable part of it was actually built of earth revetted by clay cheeks; turf cheeks are also known. Most of the eastern 16 km (10 miles) from Watling Lodge to Bo'ness was constructed in this manner, though turf was used in certain places. Some earthen sections have also been recorded at the west end of the Wall. The point of junction between the eastern earth/clay wall and the main turf rampart lay at Watling Lodge, the fortlet which guarded the gate through the Antonine Wall on the road to the north.

The reason for the use of earth and clay is more problematic. Their use suggests a lack of available turves, due either to the presence of woodland or arable land, or perhaps the grass cover was too thin to provide good turves. However, an entirely different reason has been proposed: that the difference in materials reflects an original proposal to end the Wall at Watling Lodge.

The pioneering excavators of the 1890s dug many sections across the line of the rampart. In three of these they counted as many as nineteen turf lines. Accepting the instructions of the Roman military manual, which specified a thickness of 6 inches (15 cm) for each turf, the height of the rampart would have been about 3 m (10 feet). One hundred years later, we can do little better than this suggestion. The only additional evidence has been provided by Kenneth Steer who in 1957 recorded twenty-two lines in the rampart at Bonnyside. The 1890s' excavators also offered a profile for the

Fig. 5.11 Artist's impression of the building of the Antonine Wall.
Drawn by Michael. J. Moore.

rampart. They noted a 30 degree slope at the rear. Yet while we can offer a section of the lower part of the rampart, we still have no evidence as to how the top was completed, whether there was a walkway or breastwork, for example.

A simple calculation demonstrates that turf would require to be stripped from an area 100 m (300 feet) wide from north to south along the length of the Wall in order to be able to construct a wall 3 m (10 ft) high, assuming that all the turf in closest proximity to the Wall was usable. Interestingly, in at least some sectors, the turf was not stripped from below the upcast mound before soil from the ditch was dumped on it. This may suggest that there was plentiful turf available, or simply a lack of proper cooperation between rampart builders and ditch diggers.

In front of the Wall lay a wide and deep ditch. The sides were often cut to a 30 degree slope, and sometimes the lips were marked by large stones. These may have been intended to mark the line of the ditch, or perhaps to help prevent the loose earth of the upcast mound from slipping back into the ditch. There is considerable

Fig. 5.12 The ditch at Watling Lodge, Falkirk, is very well preserved.

variation in the size of the ditch, from 4.27 m (14 ft) to 20.73 m (68 ft), though sometimes the greater width is the result of later erosion. For much of the central sector, from Bantaskine, between Falkirk and Watling Lodge, to Bar Hill the ditch averages 12 m (40 ft) wide and 4 m (12 ft) deep, though narrower widths have been recorded. East of Falkirk widths vary from 6.10 to 10.70 m (20 to 35 ft). West of Bar Hill the ditch was generally 6.10 m (20 ft) to 7.60 m (25 ft) wide. Sometimes two very different widths were recorded close together, for example at Hillhead to the east of Kirkintilloch. This may reflect the work of different legions. When the ditch narrowed, the berm tended to increase, and generally, it has been noted, the distance between the front of the rampart and the middle of the ditch remained constant.

In some places, where the rock was especially hard, the ditch was not completed. The known sectors where the soldiers failed in their duty are on Croy Hill, Bar Hill and towards the west end of the Wall at Carleith. To the east of Bar Hill, in one sector, the top soil was removed but no more, while in the adjacent sector not even this task was undertaken. On Croy Hill a causeway of undug rock lies immediately to the east of the fort, while among the crags to the west the ditch was not always completed. Yet, throughout this stretch a ditch was normally provided, even though the existence of the crags formed by the dolerite outcrops rendered it unnecessary. Today, bizarrely to our eyes, the ditch with its small upcast mound lies at the bottom of the crags in a wide natural trough, totally superfluous in view of the nature of the ground.

The material from the ditch was tipped out onto the north side and generally spread out and levelled, though this was not completed on the eastern flank of Croy Hill as is visible today. The resulting mound was much wider than the ditch, often attaining a width of 18 m (60 ft). One advantage was to heighten the north side of the ditch. Where the land fell steeply to the north, as at Watling Lodge, the mound was narrowed and the spoil heaped up to a sharper and higher profile, roughly triangular in shape.

The berm, the space between the rampart and the ditch, was normally about 6 m (20 ft) wide, but might widen to as much as 30 m

(100 ft) when the Wall crossed the difficult terrain of Croy Hill. One of the most exciting recent discoveries along the line of the Antonine Wall has been pits on the berm. Similar pits have long been known at Rough Castle, having been found during the excavations of 1903 (see fig. 8.5). There they lie in ten rows to the north of the upcast mound. The newly discovered pits have been found on the berm in several places, all in the eastern half of the Wall, but it is possible that they may yet be found elsewhere. At Garnhall, the pits were laid out in three rows and had been left open to silt naturally; in Callendar Park there were four rows; at Laurieston three, and possibly as many as five, rows. In each case, and at Rough Castle, the pits were staggered. These pits presumably contained obstacles such as stakes or branches which would have impeded movement on the berm. Those excavated between Wallsend and Newcastle on Hadrian's Wall each held two stakes.

The final linear element was the Military Way. This road ran along the whole length of the Wall and was usually located between 15 and 40 m (50 and 120 ft) south of the rampart. It was constructed of stones and gravel, in one place laid on a bed of turf. Generally a little over 5 m (16 ft) wide, it had ditches to each side to help drainage. There is some evidence to suggest that the road was constructed early in the building programme for a quarry pit to provide stone for use in its construction underlay one of the expansions attached to the rear of the Wall at Rough Castle. The Military Way formed the main road through most forts, though at these by-passes were also provided.

It has been calculated that the construction of the rampart and the Military Way and the excavation of the ditch might have taken about eight months, that is, perhaps a little over one season's work.

The various differences in the width of the ditch and rampart base and the composition of the rampart have been plotted and related to the distribution of the distance slabs in the hope that it might be possible to associate the differences to the work of different legions. It would be fair to say that this has met with only moderate success. Some differences appear to lie each side of the point where two legionary sectors met, but we cannot relate the major differences

Fig. 5.13 The Military Way in Seabegs Wood.

in the width of the ditch and in particular the break between turf and earth/clay at Watling Lodge to legionary lengths.

THE EAST END OF THE WALL

In spite of centuries of observation of the Antonine Wall and 100 years of excavation, there is still some dubiety about the location of the eastern end of the Wall. Until the late nineteenth century, it was presumed that the Wall ended at Carriden. The discovery in 1868 of a massive distance slab at Bridgeness Tower only 6 m (20 ft) from the high water mark in the Firth of Forth led Sir George Macdonald to propose this as the end of the Wall. The position has much to recommend it. A ridge of land runs down to the shore at this point and projects slightly into the estuary. The stone lay over a pit and H. M. Cadell, on whose land it was found and who published several records of its discovery, believed that the retreating Roman army had laid it in this position.

Excavation over the last thirty years in three places along the 200 m (600 ft) of the presumed line of the Wall to the west of the find spot has failed to find any trace of the structure, even of the ditch which is difficult to destroy completely. This has led Geoff Bailey to disinter the earlier arguments and propose that the Wall ended further east, closer to the fort at Carriden. He argues that the distance slab was moved to the place of its discovery during the medieval period or later in order to be broken up and reused, perhaps in the building of Bridgeness Tower. Limited investigation in 1994 on the Carriden line has, however, not located the Wall. In the circumstances, and bearing in mind the size of the distance slab which suggests that it had not been moved far, it seems better to retain the Macdonald argument for the eastern end of the Wall being beside the Bridgeness Tower. Even so, neither the distance from the River Avon to Bridgeness nor to Carriden corresponds exactly to the figure of 4,652 paces on the distance slab.

Gordon Maxwell has offered a very different proposition. Noting that the ditch is narrower east of the River Avon, and that the

Wall is not correctly aligned on each bank where it meets the river, he has suggested that the original plan was to end the Wall at this point. The higher sea level in the Roman period might offer some support to this theory as this point must have been very close to the coastline.

In conclusion, the location of the massive Bridgeness distance slab, coupled with the precise measurements of the distance slabs, which indicate detailed and comprehensive planning, might be taken to imply that the original intention was to end the Wall at Bridgeness.

FORTS AND FORTLETS: THE FIRST PLAN

Along the line of the Antonine Wall as many as seventeen forts are known. However, they relate to the rampart in different ways. Some were clearly planned or built earlier than the rampart while others were equally clearly additions. The primary forts are Mumrills, Castlecary, Balmuildy and Old Kilpatrick.

At Mumrills the Wall does a zig-zag to accommodate the fort, which appears to have been built with little wing-walls, at least to the west, to await the arrival of the rampart builders. Balmuildy also has wing-walls at the northern corners, while both it and Castlecary had stone defensive walls, the only forts on the Antonine Wall to have been so constructed. Old Kilpatrick was erected as a free-standing fort before the rampart-builders arrived.

These forts are different distances apart. Mumrills is 11.2 km (7 miles) from the presumed eastern end of the Wall at Bridgeness. Mumrills and Castlecary are 14.5 km (9 miles) apart, while 24 km (15 miles) separate Castlecary and Balmuildy. Old Kilpatrick lies 14.5 km (9 miles) beyond Balmuildy. Beyond the eastern end of the Wall sits the fort at Carriden: this could therefore be an original fort. Between Castlecary and Balmuildy two forts are contenders for the accolade of being a primary fort. Bar Hill is 9.6 km (6 miles) from Castlecary and 14.5 km (9 miles) from Balmuildy. Auchendavy lies 12.8 km (8 miles) from Castlecary and 11.2 km (7 miles) from Balmuildy. Auchendavy is therefore more central and, on that basis,

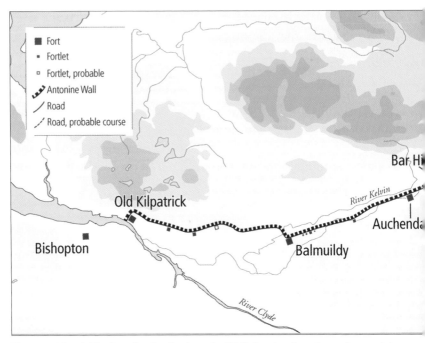

Fig. 5.14 (above) The first plan for the Antonine Wall showing the primary forts and the known fortlets.

Fig. 5.15 (right) Plan of the fort at Balmuildy. The wing-walls are visible at the northern corners of the fort.

ought to be the primary fort: it was the preference of John Gillam, who promulgated the current theory for the building of the Wall. Bar Hill, however, sits on a high eminence, which might give it a claim to primacy, and has produced evidence for two regiments which offers some support. It also, uniquely on the line of the Wall, is not attached to the rampart. Auchendavy is also markedly smaller than the other primary forts.

The average distance apart is about 13 km (8 miles). This figure occurs both on Hadrian's Wall and on the German frontier. It is roughly half the normal day's march of 23 km (14 miles) and would appear to have been a convenient distance to separate forts on the frontier itself: behind the Wall the forts remained a day's march apart.

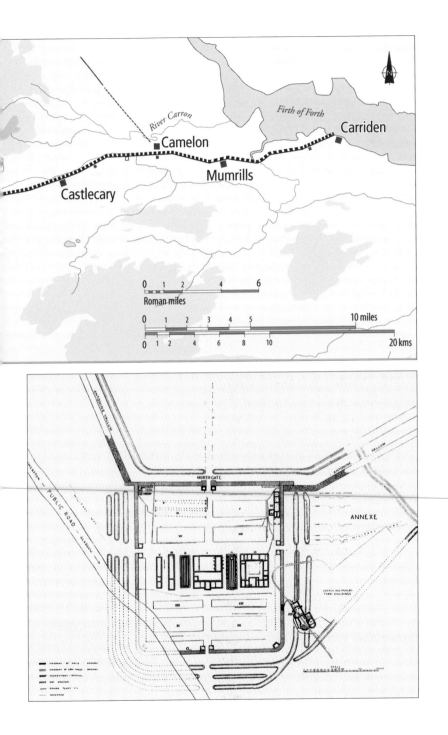

River Carron

Firth of Forth

Carriden

Camelon

Mumrills

Castlecary

Roman miles
0   1   2   4   6

0   1   2   3   4   5   10 miles

0 1 2   4   6   8   10   20 kms

ANTONINE VALLUM

ANTONINE VALLUM

PUBLIC ROAD — GLASGOW

NORTH GATE

ANNEXE

EASTER DALFRULZIE
FARM BUILDINGS

| | SIZE IN HECTARES | | SIZE IN ACRES | | DISTANCE BETWEEN |
	EXTERNAL	INTERNAL	EXTERNAL	INTERNAL	FORTS
Carriden	c.1.76	c.1.6	c.4.4	c. 4.0	
					12.4 km/7¾ miles
Mumrills	2.9	2.6	7.3	6.5	
					14.5 km/9 miles
Castlecary	1.56	1.4	3.9	3.5	
					12.8 km/8 miles
Auchendavy	1.2	1.09	3.0	2.7	
					9.6 km/6 miles
Bar Hill	1.4	1.28	3.5	3.2	
					14.5 km/9 miles
					11.2 km/7 miles
Balmuildy	1.72	1.6	4.34	4.0	
					14.5 km/9 miles
Old Kilpatrick	1.88	1.7	4.7	4.2	

Table 4 The primary forts on the Antonine Wall

These forts, like those on Hadrian's Wall, were all of sufficient size to hold a complete auxiliary unit. Mumrills is considerably larger than all other forts on the Wall. This presumably reflects the placing here of a cavalry regiment, the *ala I Tungrorum*: 500 men and their horses always required a larger base than an infantry unit of equivalent size such as are recorded at Bar Hill and Old Kilpatrick. The names of the regiments based at Carriden and Balmuildy are not known, but at the latter barrack-blocks for only 480 men were provided. The situation at Castlecary is very strange. Two large 1,000-strong infantry cohorts are attested here, while the number of inscriptions recording legionaries leaves little doubt but to conclude that a third force was present at some time. Each cohort contained 800 men, too many for the fort, therefore some soldiers from both cohorts must have been outposted elsewhere.

Fig. 5.16 The fortlet at Kinneil, near Bo'ness, from the air.

Some of these soldiers may have been sent to man the fortlets along the Wall. The first fortlet was discovered in 1894 but for long was thought to be unique, a special post to protect the gate through the Wall on the road leading north at Watling Lodge. However, shortly after World War II, two fortlets were located as a result of aerial photography and a third through excavation. This last fortlet lay on Golden Hill, Duntocher, and was found to have been built before the rampart-builders arrived at the site (see fig. 2.11). A second fortlet, Wilderness Plantation, was examined in 1965–6: it was constructed at the same time as the rampart.

So matters stood for many years until, in 1975, it was suggested that these four known fortlets were not isolated discoveries but formed part of a pattern of fortlets along the whole line of the Wall, there being one at roughly every mile. Archaeologists were eager to test this new theory and within five years five new fortlets had been located. The course of the Wall suggests the location of other possibilities. It would appear that the Gillam hypothesis has been triumphantly proved.

The fortlets were small enclosures, measuring about 21 by 18 m (70 by 60 ft), very similar to the size of the milecastles on Hadrian's Wall. Indeed, they are similar in other ways for a road passed through the fortlet leading to a gate in the north rampart, the Antonine Wall itself. The side walls of the fortlet were of turf placed on a stone base, and some have been found to contain small timber buildings, presumably barrack-blocks, with hearths. They are usually protected by at least one ditch, unlike the milecastles on the southern frontier which are rarely protected by ditches. With the exceptions of Duntocher and Cleddans, the known fortlets are all contemporary with the construction of the rampart: these two were erected before the rampart.

Each fortlet had a north gate but one important additional element was lacking, a causeway over the ditch in front of the gate. This problem is not unique to the Antonine Wall because the situation was similar on Hadrian's Wall. There, however, recent survey has suggested that original causeways may have been later removed following changes in plan during the construction of the Wall. The possible locations of causeways on the Antonine Wall have not been investigated, but, taken at face value, it is surprising that none existed because otherwise the gates would have been largely superfluous. Perhaps, again, a change in plan led to their removal.

Hadrian's Wall and the Antonine frontier in Germany had one other structure erected on their lines which, so far, has not been discovered on the Antonine Wall, namely towers. Towers, called turrets on Hadrian's Wall, were erected at one-third of a mile intervals. If towers existed on the Antonine Wall, they would presumably have been constructed of timber and their remains may lie, undiscovered, within the thickness of the rampart; timber towers were normally about 3 m (10 ft) square and would be hidden within a rampart base 4.4 m (15 ft) wide unless found by chance. Only in one location, at the east end of Callendar Park, Falkirk, has evidence been found for a timber post. A post-hole, 30 cm (1 ft) square, was found above the south kerb of the rampart, its base directly on the kerb stones. No other post-hole was found, though a large stone in the rampart base was tentatively interpreted as a post-pad. Seven metres (22 ft 9 in) behind the rampart at this point was a hearth and around it was found some pottery and burnt bones. The excavator, Geoff Bailey, suggested that there may have been a bothy here, its structural timbers resting directly on the ground, used by the soldiers who manned the tower.

If normal towers have yet to be positively identified, the Antonine Wall possesses two types of structures not found on any other frontier, the 'expansions' and the small enclosures.

'Expansions' have long been known. They occur in pairs. There are two to the east and a further two to the west of Rough Castle and two on the western slope of Croy Hill. The most completely excavated example, Bonnyside East, beside Rough Castle, was found to consist of a stone base 5.18 m (17 ft) square on which was erected a turf superstructure, presumably to the same height as the rampart. While the stone base was laid separately from the Antonine Wall base, the turves in the superstructures of the rampart and the expansion overlapped, suggesting that they were erected at the same time. This was not the case at one of the 'expansions' on Croy Hill where there was no continuous stone base and the turves were laid on the ground after the Antonine Wall rampart had been constructed.

We can describe an 'expansion', but determining its function is another matter. The discovery of a considerable amount of burnt wood and burnt turf around the base of Bonnyside East was presumed to have come from fires erected on a platform at the top of the 'expansion'. The pairing of the towers and their location would support the hypothesis that they were beacon-platforms. The pair on each side of Rough Castle face north towards the outpost forts, while those on the western slope of Croy Hill look southwards towards the hinterland fort at Bothwellhaugh within the modern Strathclyde Country Park. What is required is some experimental archaeology to find out from what distance separate lights on the platforms would be

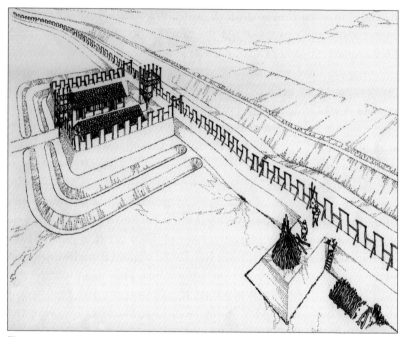

Fig. 5.17 Artist's impression of a fortlet and 'expansion'. Drawn by Michael. J. Moore.

distinguishable. Certainly, fires on such platforms could only have sent the simplest of signals. It remains possible to offer a different interpretation of the archaeological evidence. Fires lit by soldiers at the base of the platform, perhaps in the corner of the rampart and platform, are likely to have burnt the adjacent turves. Furthermore, the climate would have restricted their use. Other explanations are, however, difficult to produce. It is highly unlikely that they were bases for the provision of artillery. It is difficult to see why these particular places would have been chosen for catapults and, in any case, auxiliary soldiers were not normally issued with artillery at this time.

A further equally enigmatic structure was discovered as recently as 1978. In studying aerial photographs, Gordon Maxwell noticed three small enclosures immediately to the rear of the Wall at Wilderness Plantation. The spacings between the three enclosures and the fortlet are about 260 m (805 ft), 285 m (903 ft) and 295 m (907 ft). These distances are rather less than one-sixth of a Roman mile, but the variation was too great to confirm an intention for such a spacing.

One enclosure was subsequently excavated and found to consist of a single ditch surrounding a slight turf rampart and enclosing an area about 5.5 m (18 ft) square. This is exactly the size of a turret on Hadrian's Wall. No entrance was found and no structure within the enclosure, so its purpose remains a mystery. We can at least place it within the building sequence. To each side of the enclosure, the turf was stripped for use in the Wall, but not from under the enclosure. This would suggest that the enclosure was planned from the first.

These are not the only structures on the Antonine Wall which cannot be fully explained. At Inveravon, the edge of a platform was discovered in 1991. It butted against the rear of the rampart base and while secondary there was a possibility that the turf superstructure of the two bonded at a higher level. This was tentatively interpreted as an 'expansion', but too little is known of the structure for the identification to be confirmed. Moreover, the platform was 7.8 m (25 ft 7 in) long compared to the largest 'expansion' bases elsewhere which are no more than 5.18 m (17 ft) wide. An alternative suggestion, therefore, is that it was the base of the rampart of a fort or its annexe at Inveravon.

A platform, though of a different design, was found to the rear of the Wall at Tollpark in 1979. This platform was only 1.8 m (5 ft 10 in) wide but was 12 m (39 ft 4 in) long. It was not original for in places it overlay turf which had fallen from the adjacent rampart. However, the platform itself did not form the base of a turf stack. An area of burning was recorded at its eastern end, but its function could not be determined.

The blueprint for the Antonine Wall would therefore appear to have been for a rampart of turf or clay and earth from sea to sea, with forts at fairly regular intervals and fortlets in between at intervals of roughly one Roman mile. No towers have been found, but both 'expansions', possibly serving as beacon-platforms, and small enclosures of tower size are known. This original blueprint for the Antonine Wall, however, was amended before completion, and it is to that which we must now turn.

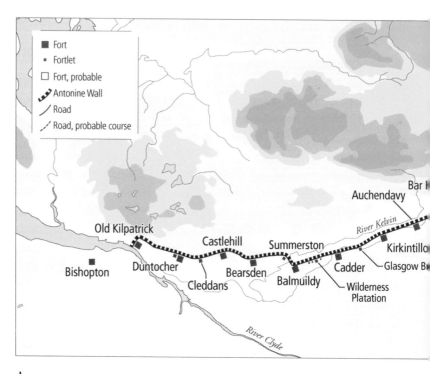

A MAJOR CHANGE IN DESIGN:
NEW FORTS AND REDUNDANT FORTLETS

The earliest excavations on the line of the Wall demonstrated that some forts were later than the rampart. This was clear at Rough Castle where in 1903 it was revealed that the ramparts of the fort were wider than the Antonine Wall rampart and built at a higher level. We can now see that Westerwood, Croy Hill and Cadder were also secondary. In all other cases, insufficient evidence survives to determine whether the fort is primary or secondary.

It is immediately obvious that the average distance now between forts was about 3.5 km (2¼ miles). Bearsden is out of position, with no obvious explanation: there seems to be no topographical reason why it could not have lain 1.6 km (1 mile) to the east. The long gaps between Carriden and Inveravon, and between Rough Castle and Castlecary, have led some to believe there are missing forts. While that may be the case, field work and excavation have failed to reveal

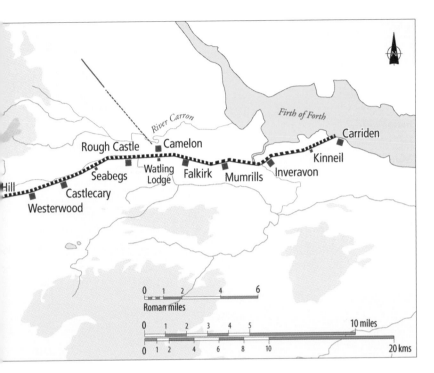

Fig. 5.18 The second scheme for the Antonine Wall.

any fort in either supposed location. It is possible that none existed.

Another feature revealed by Table 5 is that, with the exceptions of Castlehill and Kirkintilloch, the new forts are all smaller than the primary forts. Further, with the exception of Castlehill's neighbour, Duntocher, those in the western half of the Wall are all larger than those to the east.

We know even less about the auxiliary units based at the secondary forts than we do about those at the primary stations. The Sixth Cohort of Nervians was based at Rough Castle, where it left a record of its building work. The Fourth Cohort of Gauls erected an altar at Castlehill to the Goddesses of the Parade-ground. Otherwise the only soldiers whose presence is attested through inscriptions are legionaries. These occur at Westerwood, Croy Hill and Auchendavy. It is surprising to find legionaries at such small frontier posts, yet the evidence strongly suggests that they were based here. The wife of a

| | SIZE IN HECTARES | | SIZE IN ACRES | | DISTANCE BETWEEN |
	EXTERNAL	INTERNAL	EXTERNAL	INTERNAL	FORTS
Carriden	c.1.76	c.1.6	c.4.4	c.4.0	
Inveravon					8 km/5 miles
Mumrills	2.9	2.6	7.3	6.5	3.2 km/2 miles
Falkirk					3.2 km/2 miles
Rough Castle	0.6	0.5	1.5	1.0	4 km/2½ miles
Castlecary	1.56	1.4	3.9	3.5	5.6 km/3½ miles
Westerwood	0.96	0.8	2.4	2.0	3.2 km/2 miles
Croy Hill	0.8	0.6	2.0	1.5	2.8 km/1¾ miles
Bar Hill	1.4	1.28	3.5	3.2	2.8 km/1¾ miles
Auchendavy	1.2	1.09	3.0	2.7	3.2 km/2 miles
Kirkintilloch	c.1.3	c.1.4	c.3.2	c.3.5	2.8 km/1¾ miles
Cadder	1.1	1.34	3.35	2.8	4 km/2⅜ miles
Balmuildy	1.72	1.6	4.34	4.0	3.5 km/2¼ miles
Bearsden	1.2	0.95	2.8	2.4	4.2 km/3¾ miles
Castlehill	c.1.41	c.1.28	c.3.5	c.3.2	2.3 km/1½ miles
Duntocher	0.26	0.2	0.66	0.5	3.2 km/2 miles
Old Kilpatrick	1.88	1.7	4.7	4.2	3.5 km/2¼ miles

Table 5 The forts on the Antonine Wall (primary forts in bold)

Fig. 5.19 Rough Castle fort from the air. The Antonine Wall crosses the photograph diagonally from bottom left. The fort and its annexe are delineated by ditches. Top right are the banks of a small field system.

centurion is recorded at Westerwood. Three building stones and the tombstone of a legionary occur at Croy Hill (see fig. 7.9), while Auchendavy has furnished no less than four altars dedicated by a centurion of the Second Legion (see fig. 7.6), two tombstones and a building stone. Perhaps the manning of the Antonine Wall overstretched the resources of the army of Britain, leading to the stationing of legionaries on the frontier. However, we may note that a legionary detachment was based at Housesteads on Hadrian's Wall for a time, while several milecastles along that frontier have also produced inscriptions recording legionaries.

Mumrills	First Cavalry Regiment of Tungrians and Second Cohort of Thracians
Rough Castle	Sixth Cohort of Nervians
Castlecary	First cohort of Tungrians, First Cohort of Vardullians and soldiers of legions II and VI
Westerwood	soldiers of legion VI
Croy Hill	soldiers of legion VI
Bar Hill	First Cohort of Baetasians and First Cohort of Hamians
Auchendavy	soldiers of legion II
Balmuildy	plan suggests a 480-strong cohort
Bearsden	barracks suggest the presence of cavalry
Castlehill	Fourth Cohort of Gauls
Old Kilpatrick	First Cohort of Baetasians

Table 6 The units attested at Antonine Wall forts

The existence of two auxiliary units at some sites may be explained by the change in plan and the addition of forts to the Wall. Two of the primary forts, Mumrills and Castlecary, have furnished evidence for the presence of two auxiliary regiments. Two units are also recorded at Bar Hill, which strengthens its claim to be a primary fort, for no secondary fort has furnished evidence for two auxiliary regiments. It seems possible that the addition of new forts to the Wall might have resulted in changes to the original distribution of units and perhaps also some of the internal amendments which have been noted in many forts. These include the rebuilding of the headquarters and commanding officer's house at Mumrills and work on these buildings and on barracks in other forts.

The placing of extra forts on the frontier had an effect on the fortlets. In some cases, existing fortlets were replaced by forts. This occurred at Croy Hill, Duntocher, and possibly Rough Castle. In other instances, the function of the fortlet appears to have changed. At Wilderness Plantation, the earlier timber buildings were removed and most of the interior surface of the fortlet covered by a layer of cobbles; this surface extended up to the north gate, though not to the area to each side, suggesting that the gate remained in use. At Kinneil, the interior, in at least the northern half, was covered with a layer of cobbles and flags. Here, however, the north gate appears to have gone out of use, with a culvert cut through the position of the east post-holes of the gate and a hearth placed in the middle of the entrance. At Seabegs, too, a secondary layer of cobbling was recorded.

The decision to place additional forts on the Antonine Wall occurred before the original plan for its construction was completed. The Wall building had not yet reached Cleddans, just over 5 km (3 miles) from the western terminal because the fortlet here predates the rampart. Cleddans is 1.6 km (1 mile) west of Castlehill, the point at which the unit of measurement of the construction of the rampart changed from paces to feet and the method of dividing up the work also changed. Now, instead of each legion being allocated a stretch 4.8 km (3 miles) or more long, the remaining four miles was divided into six sections, two separate sections being assigned to each of the three legions. It is difficult to avoid the conclusion that the change in allocating work to the legions is linked in some way to the decision to place extra forts on the Wall line. One effect of the different division of work was to lead to the erection of many more distance slabs in the western four miles of the Wall.

ANNEXES

Annexes are known outside several forts along the Wall. These have long been recognised, but their purpose is little understood. Several contained the regimental bath-house. Some have produced evidence for industrial activity. Perhaps they housed activities regarded as too dangerous to be undertaken within the fort, though forts are known to have contained both bath-houses and workshops. Possibly they provided shelter for troops in transit.

Annexes occur at the primary forts at Mumrills, Castlecary and Balmuildy, as well as at the secondary forts at Rough Castle, Bearsden and Duntocher. Annexes probably existed at other forts,

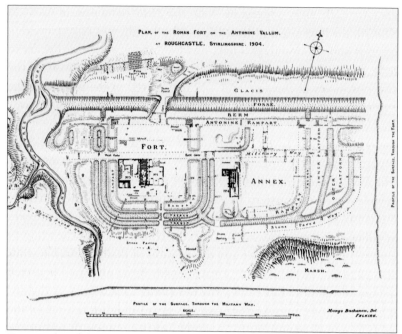

Fig. 5.20 Plan of the fort at Rough Castle.

but the evidence is not so clear-cut. In several cases it is apparent that the annexes were not planned from the first but were an addition to the fort. At Mumrills, the three western ditches of the fort were filled in when the annexe was constructed. It has been argued that the filling of the east ditches at Falkirk could be explained in the same way, though the annexe has not been located. At Castlecary, at least two of the east fort ditches were infilled when the annexe was constructed, possibly one at Rough Castle, and certainly two at Balmuildy. At Bearsden, an originally large enclosure appears to have been divided into fort and annexe before any of the fort's internal buildings, apart from the bath-house, were erected. Even the bath-house had not been completed and the change in plan resulted in its demolition and replacement by a building on a different alignment. Finally, at tiny Duntocher the ditches, as at Bearsden, enclosed both fort and annexe. Unfortunately it is not clear from the excavation report whether the annexe rampart butted against the fort's corner, as the excavator believed, or the relationship was the same as at Bearsden with a single larger enclosure subsequently subdivided.

We can see, as in other aspects of the construction of the Antonine Wall, a distinction between the western and eastern parts. The forts including and to the east of Balmuildy were all constructed before annexes were added. At Bearsden, few, if any, of the fort's buildings had been completed before there was a radical change in plan. At Duntocher, on the other hand, the annexe was more closely integrated into the basic plan and suggests that fort and annexe had been designed more or less at the same time. One possibility is that a larger fort was planned here but, as at Bearsden, had been subsequently divided into fort and annexe.

The construction of the annexe at Mumrills appears to be dated by pottery recovered from the backfilled fort ditches. The date determined for the pottery is 155–60. At Inveravon, the base identified as an 'expansion' was subsumed within an enclosure, presumably either a fort or its annexe. Most of a samian vessel and part of a mixing bowl made by potters who worked within the period 155 to 190 date this second phase.

It has been suggested that the annexes were only added to forts once an earlier plan to construct a protective earthwork to the rear of the Wall on the lines of the Vallum on Hadrian's Wall was abandoned. This, however, cannot be proved.

A REVIEW OF THE BUILDING PROJECT

The original plan for the Antonine Wall was for a rampart and ditch with six forts averaging 13 km (8 miles) apart and fortlets between at intervals of a little more than 1.6 km (1 mile); the Military Way, 'expansions'/beacon-platforms and small enclosures probably formed part of the same plan. The appearance of the name of the governor Lollius Urbicus on two inscriptions at the primary fort at Balmuildy indicates that work on building the Wall had already started by the presumed date of his departure from Britain in 142. Balmuildy was structurally earlier than the rampart and it is possible

Fig. 5.21 Artist's impression of the fort and annexe at Bearsden. Drawn by Michael. J. Moore.

that construction of the linear elements of the Wall had not been started before Urbicus left Britain. It would appear that it was considered unnecessary for any other governor's name to appear on the distance slabs. None of the other inscriptions from the Antonine Wall is dated within the reign of Antoninus Pius.

Before the rampart was completed, it was decided to add at least eleven forts to the frontier line, some replacing fortlets; it was probably at the same time that the other fortlets lost their internal buildings. Working from the east, the rampart-builders had probably passed Bearsden, but not yet reached Cleddans when the decision to add more forts was taken. At Castlehill, within this sector, the method of dividing up work on the rampart and the unit of measurement were changed. A link therefore seems possible.

Fig. 5.22 Coin of Antoninus Pius issued in 154/5 showing *Britannia* supposedly dejected.

At some stage it was decided to add annexes to forts. This occurred before the internal buildings at Bearsden were erected and probably before the fort at Duntocher was built. The only dating evidence comes from the eastern end of the Wall. Pottery found at Mumrills and Inveravon suggests that the annexes there were not constructed until after about 155. Other annexes could have been built earlier. This seems likely, otherwise the evidence from Duntocher, where the annexe appears to be earlier than the rampart, might be taken to imply that part of the Antonine Wall's rampart lay unfinished until the late 150s.

There is insufficient dating evidence from the Antonine Wall to confirm many of these suggestions. Nevertheless, it would appear that following the start of construction in 142, the Antonine Wall was still being modified over a dozen years later. Is it possible to offer any explanation for this long, drawn-out building programme?

The first possibility is that it simply took twelve years to build the Antonine Wall and all its attendant forts and their annexes. This seems unlikely. While we have no direct evidence for the length of time it would take the Roman army in Britain to build a frontier or even a fort, the circumstantial evidence suggests that it would be a speedier undertaking than twelve years. The 20-ha (50-acre) legionary fortress at Inchtuthil on the River Tay appears to have been erected in no more than two seasons in the late first century while the nineteenth-century engineers offered quite a tight building programme for the construction of Hadrian's Wall.

An alternative view is that work was disrupted by other events. A coin issued in 154–5 shows *Britannia*, the personification of the province, seated and resting her head on her hands (see fig. 5.22). This pose has been interpreted as indicating that the peace of the province had just been disturbed by fighting. It has also been described simply as a variant on the depiction of *Britannia* on earlier coinage, or the result of poor craftsmanship, perhaps linked to the production of the coin in Britain – they are relatively frequent finds on British sites but rare on the Continent. There does, however, appear to be agreement that the coin was issued to commemorate a victory in Britain. Fighting would have occurred in the year or years preceding the issue of the coin and could have had an impact on the building of the Antonine Wall.

A further proposition is that the delay was caused by troops being sent from Britain to partake in the war in Mauretania fought between 145 and 150. The fighting certainly sucked in troops from many of the European provinces of the empire. The evidence for a British contingent, however, is based not on inscriptions but on the appearance at this time of African cooking styles in forts on the Antonine Wall, indicative of a close connection (see Appendix IV). We may also note that part of at least one other unit was absent from Britain during the building of the Antonine Wall, the Second Cohort of Tungrians, which was in Raetia (modern southern Germany), and it may not have been unique.

Five years, from 150 to 155, would appear to be a long time for the final stage of the building work. However, the dates are only approximate. If the war did not end until 150, troops may not have returned to Britain until the following year, while the date for the pottery, by its very nature, cannot be accurate and may be a little earlier than 'about 155'. Work may then have been interrupted by fighting on the northern frontier as indicated by the coin issue. A minimum of thirteen or fourteen years for this particular building project might seem excessive, but work on Hadrian's Wall started in

122 and was still in progress fifteen years later. The willingness of the Roman army to leave their northern frontier in a part-finished state for a dozen years, does, though, have an implication for how we understand the relationship between the Romans and their neighbours.

These changes may also have had an impact on the distribution of troops along the frontier. Although the decision to build more forts on the Wall may have resulted in some units being moved from one fort to another, later events may have been equally instrumental in bringing about such movements. In fact, these several disruptions would help to explain why Castlecary had as many as three different units recorded there.

YEAR	EVENT
139	Rebuilding at Corbridge
142	Victory celebrated; Balmuildy built?
143	Wall from Castlehill to Seabegs built with primary forts, fortlets, 'expansions', small enclosures and Military Way
144	Wall from Seabegs to Bo'ness built with primary forts, fortlets, 'expansions' and Military Way
144/5	Building of secondary forts began; fortlets amended; annexes started to be added to forts? Wall from Castlehill to Old Kilpatrick may have been built
145–50	Some troops sent to fight in Mauretania? Building work on Wall slowed or even ceased
151?	Troops return to Britain
151+	Work recommences on the Wall
154–5	Coin issued showing *Britannia* seated with her head bowed indicating a victory in Britain
about 155+	Annexes added to forts (work may have started earlier); Bearsden divided into fort and annexe; Duntocher fort built; Wall from Castlehill to Old Kilpatrick built if not earlier

Table 7 A possible timetable for building the Wall

It must be emphasised that this proposed timetable is very speculative. It cannot be proved that British troops took part in the Mauretanian war. The fighting on the northern frontier depends on a single coin issue, about which there is still discussion, and is not corroborated by other evidence. There may be a different explanation for the late construction of the annexe at Mumrills, while the evidence from Inveravon came from a single narrow trench. No link can be proved between the change of the unit of measurement and the decision to add more forts to the frontier. The best that can be said is that the draft timetable does appear to fit all these disparate pieces of evidence.

VI

MILITARY DEPLOYMENT

There are on this wall ... a series of forts or stations.

———————

J. HORSLEY,
Britannia Romana (London 1732), 158

After the above review of the building of the Antonine Wall, it may be difficult to conceive of a time when there was a settled pattern of military deployment, when work was not still in progress, when forts were complete, when units were not moving to a new fort. Yet, forts were completed and, we presume, occupied.

THE ARMY OF THE WALL

As completed, the Antonine Wall contained a greater concentration of troops proportionately than was the case on Hadrian's Wall. Spread amongst its seventeen or so forts were 6,000–7,000 soldiers, whilst the total number of troops based on Hadrian's Wall, twice as long, was approximately 8,000.

The troops who were stationed in the forts along the Wall were mainly infantry. Only one example of the normal work-horse of the frontier army, the 500-strong infantry and cavalry unit, is attested, at Castlehill towards the west end of the Wall. The only cavalry regiment lay at Mumrills 5 km (3 miles) from the road north at

Camelon, which may be significant. There may be a simple reason for the relative lack of cavalry: the nature of the countryside to the north. The broad and boggy valley of the River Kelvin and the low-lying, and no doubt wet, ground north of the easternmost 9 km (6 miles) was not good country for the operation of cavalry.

Another point may be made about the troops on the Wall. There are more forts in the western half of the Wall and, with the sole exception of Mumrills, they are larger than those to the east. This may reflect the protection afforded to the eastern half of the Wall by the outpost forts to the north. Still, the western forts faced onto a landscape which appears to have supported relatively few people at the time, the Campsie Fells. Over the last sixty years the area has been twice surveyed by RCAHMS, but few prehistoric settlements were found. The answer to this conundrum may be that fewer troops were needed in populated areas because the local people would largely govern themselves and a settled farming community would not take kindly to troublemakers, especially from outside the area, because they would have a very clear appreciation of the reaction of the Roman army to insurrection: the sacking and burning of villages, perhaps even the taking of the local inhabitants into slavery.

On this model, it was the areas which were largely uninhabited, such as the hills to the north of the Wall, which would have required extra troops to patrol them, to maintain watch and ward over the frontier zone. This may seem fanciful, but the same phenomenon has been recognised on Hadrian's Wall. There, there was a greater concentration of troops in the central sector, facing the largely uninhabited areas known today as the Waste of Spadeadam. Aerial photography is producing evidence for more settlements in some areas, in particular north of Housesteads, but the picture remains very patchy.

Outpost forts, hinterland forts

The Antonine Wall sat firmly within a military landscape. Stretching beyond the Wall, as far as Bertha on the River Tay just upstream

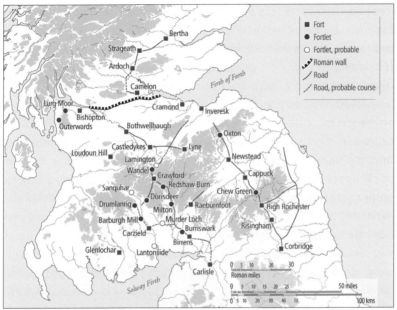

Fig. 6.1 Military deployment in north Britain during the reign of Antoninus.

Fig. 6.2 The fortlet at Lurg Moor from the air.

from modern Perth, lay a string of at least four outpost forts. Their purpose is not entirely clear. As the Antonine Wall was not necessarily the provincial boundary but merely followed the most convenient line for its purpose, the function of the units in the outpost forts may have been to protect those provincials living beyond it. This may seem to be preferable to regarding the purpose of the troops in the outpost forts as being to give advance warning of attack: that was the role of scouts. Something of a difference in function or role between the regiments based on the Wall and those in the forts to the north is hinted at through the position of one outpost fort immediately north of the Wall, at Camelon beside the road through the Wall, but that difference is not easy for us to determine.

We are, it is to be hoped, on rather safer ground when considering the forts to east and west of the Wall. On the high ground overlooking the Clyde estuary to the west sit two fortlets, at Lurg Moor and Outerwards, both in superb vantage points. To the east, Cramond lies 18 km (11 miles) beyond the Wall and Inveresk a further 18 km (11 miles) to the east. Fife, on the north shore of the Firth of Forth, seems very close and it is not surprising that it was considered necessary to place forts here.

Forts lay on the main roads leading south into the province. The purpose of the troops here may have been two-fold: to police the new provincials and to help protect them from attack. There are two particular differences between the arrangements made at this time and the deployment of forces in the Scottish Lowlands in the first century. In the earlier period, a large fort was placed in each of the main river valleys. The arrangement was not repeated in the second century, with the exception of Newstead in Tweeddale. The reason for the different treatment of Tweeddale is not clear: it may relate to the existence of a large local population. It is interesting, and coincidental, to note the nearby major pre-Roman hill fort on Eildon Hill North, the prestigious abbey of Melrose and that today the headquarters of the local authority lies in the nearest town, indicating the strategic importance of the Newstead area over many centuries.

The second change is the greater use of fortlets throughout the Lowlands in the second century. The result is that the density of military installations appears greater in Antonine Scotland than in Agricolan Scotland and in that way the pattern relates to the greater density of forts and other structures on the Antonine Wall.

THE FORTS

The troops on duty on the Antonine Wall were, as we have seen, housed in a series of forts placed roughly 3.5 km (2¼ miles) apart. The forts vary considerably in size from tiny Duntocher to Mumrills, capable of holding a cavalry regiment. This is in contrast to both Hadrian's Wall and the German frontier where each fort appears to have held a complete unit and, as a result, they were more similar in size. The internal arrangements also varied more than on the other two frontiers. Yet, Bearsden, apparently without a head-quarters building and with gaps between several of the buildings, was laid out within a grid based on the *actus*, a unit of measurement 120 Roman feet (35 m) long (see fig. 6.5). The plan, which appears to us rather haphazard, was clearly carefully designed.

Each fort formed a small enclosure protected by a rampart and several ditches. At two forts the rampart was a stone wall, but elsewhere it was of turf, sometimes with a stone base, and occasionally noticeably wider than the Antonine Wall rampart.

The number of ditches ranged from one to four. They were generally broken at the fort gates, but in some instances the ditches continued across the front of the entrance without a gap. At Bar Hill, unusually, an extra short ditch provided additional defence at the east gate.

The gates were normally simple, single portal entrances, often without flanking towers. Corner towers are known but were not always provided.

Each fort contained the normal range of buildings. In the centre was the headquarters building. To the right, in the position of pre-eminence, generally stood the commanding officer's house. In earlier

Fig. 6.3 An artist's impression of the fort at Bar Hill looking north-west. The headquarters building lies in the centre with the commanding officer's house to its left and a granary to the right. The bath-house occupies the north-west corner. The rest of the area is taken up by barrack-blocks. Drawn by Michael J. Moore.

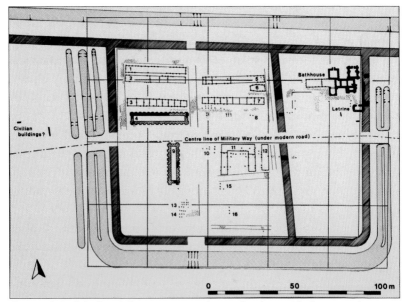

Fig. 6.4 Plan of the fort and annexe at Bearsden overlain by a grid of squares of 120 Roman feet.

forts the granaries usually lay on the other side of the headquarters but on the Antonine Wall they often flanked it with one on each side, though in two cases, Croy and Bearsden, a granary lay in the forward part of the fort. These three buildings were usually of stone. Most of the remainder of the fort was occupied by barrack-blocks and storehouses. All of these were built of wood.

The materials used to build the forts were obtained locally. The stone was sandstone, widely available in central Scotland. Timber was also freely available. The main timbers in the barracks at Bar Hill were oak. Willow was used to make a tiny wooden box and probably water pipes. Other trees represented at the fort include alder, ash, birch, elm, hawthorn, hazel, pine and rowan. Alder, hazel and willow branches were used at Bearsden to create a fence probably as a breastwork on the fort rampart. The roofs of stone buildings might have been of tile, but others were probably of thatch. Nails may have been imported. A lead pig found on the site of the fort at Kirkintilloch in the early nineteenth century may also have been an import, the lead to be used for pipes.

The number of barrack-blocks is often a guide to the size of the unit stationed at a particular fort. The six barrack-blocks at Balmuildy indicate a small 500-strong infantry unit. The small barrack-blocks at Bearsden, apparently with only eight rooms for the soldiers, were probably occupied by cavalry.

On the Antonine Wall, the regimental bath-house was often inside the fort. In one case, Balmuildy, this was replaced by an external bath-house, and at several forts bath-houses were erected in the annexe. Latrines, where they are known, tend to be associated with the bath-house.

This, then, was the core range of facilities common to nearly every fort and we can turn to examining each building in detail.

THE HEADQUARTERS BUILDING

Always in the centre of the fort, the headquarters building has a special place in the history of research on the Antonine Wall. During

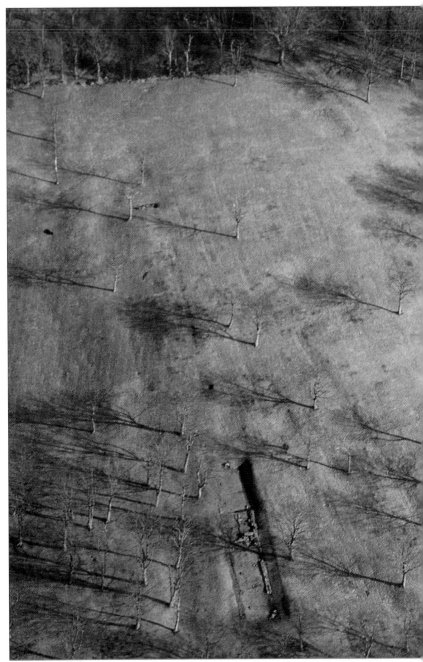

Fig. 6.5 The fort at Bar Hill from the air looking east. The headquarters building lies in the centre of the fort with the bath-house towards the bottom left corner.

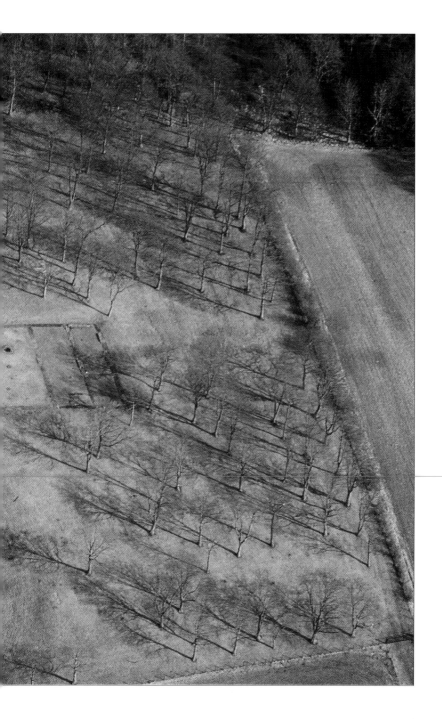

Fig. 6.6 The building inscription found at Rough Castle in 1903 which demonstrated that the Roman name of its headquarters building was *principia*.

excavations at Rough Castle in 1903, an inscription was found in the well of the headquarters building. It provided for the first time the correct name of the building type in which it was discovered. Unfortunately the inscription was broken into three parts and not complete, so the word only survives as PRI[...]PIA. Nevertheless, it is clear that the word must be restored as PRINCIPIA. Until that date, it was believed that the Latin name of the headquarters building was *praetorium*, because that is the name which appears in all our literary sources, being the name of the commanding officer's tent, which also served as his headquarters on campaign. This new piece of information was followed by the discovery of other inscriptions and we now know that the building's cross-hall was termed the *basilica*, and the shrine at the back, the *aedes*.

There were three main parts to a headquarters building. The front half, or thereabouts, formed a courtyard. Round three sides were covered loggias. Here perhaps notices were pinned giving information about the duties of soldiers: we know that such lists were prepared and kept by the army. Often a well lay in the open part of the courtyard. Perhaps this was a protected supply; possibly the water was required for use in religious ceremonies.

Beyond the courtyard lay a hall running across the whole width of the building. At one end was a dais or tribunal. This was the assembly hall for the unit. Perhaps this was the place where the commanding officer stood each morning to issue the orders for the day. Possibly here also the commanding officer administered justice over the civilians who lived on the fort's territory.

At the rear of the headquarters building usually lay five rooms. The central one was the shrine, or *aedes*. Here, in some forts, though not on the Antonine Wall, lay a strong-room. The presence of a permanent guard at the headquarters building was presumably one reason for the location of the strong-room here and, although we have no direct evidence from the Wall, we may assume that the regimental treasury was kept here.

The other four rooms were used by the clerks of the unit. These included the staff who maintained the files on individual soldiers and horses, created worksheets, recorded the ordering and delivery of supplies, prepared returns to Rome on the strength of the unit and so on. Some of the clerks also looked after the soldiers' pay and savings. These could be quite substantial: a revolt on the Rhine frontier in the first century had been funded out of the savings of two legions.

THE COMMANDING OFFICER'S HOUSE

The commanding officer stood apart from his men. He was a member of the aristocracy and probably brought his wife and family with him: certainly he would have brought slaves.

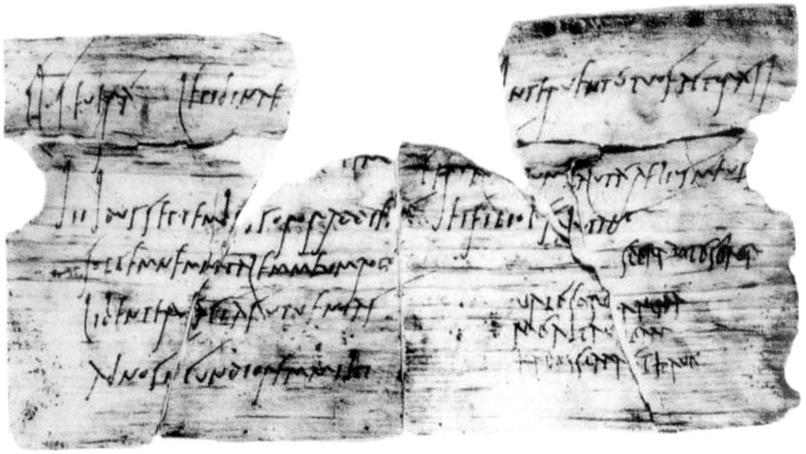

Fig. 6.7 This letter found at Vindolanda is an invitation to a birthday party to Sulpicia Lepidina, wife of the commanding officer, from another army wife.

He was provided with a house commensurate with his social status. The basic plan, even in a small fort such as Rough Castle, was a courtyard surrounded by four ranges of rooms. The commander of the largest regiment on the Wall at Mumrills, however, had a much larger house, with his own bath-house.

The Vindolanda writing tablets shed light on the commanding officer's family. Letters survive between the wives of two commanding officers. They write about birthday parties and other celebrations, and about ailments. The women were most careful to obtain the permission of their husbands before they went to see their friends. Shoes found in the commanding officer's house indicate that one family living there had children aged about two, four or five and over seven.

Children's shoes have also been found in some of the forts on the Antonine Wall. The 1905 excavations at Bar Hill produced at least sixty-seven women's shoes and over thirty belonging to children or youths. A small number of shoes belonging to women, youths and children were also recovered from Balmuildy and Castlecary. At all three sites, the shoes were found in rubbish pits or dumped in ditches, so we have no hint of where their owners were living.

Fig. 6.8 Shoes found in the fort at Bar Hill.

GRANARIES

Each fort was provided with one or two granaries. These were usually stone-built, but timber granaries occur on the Wall. Tacitus stated in the *Agricola* that each fort should have sufficient supplies to last a year. Wheat and barley were imported to be ground at the fort. Wheat was probably mainly made into bread, while barley might have been used in porridge, gruel or soup. Barley found in the sewage at Bearsden was contaminated with weevils. As a result, our belief that barley was normally fed to horses and used as a punishment ration for troops may require revision. Ovens have been found in several forts and querns in nearly all.

While corn was a major element in the diet, soldiers also ate meat, fruit and vegetables. Cattle, sheep and pig were eaten, as at Bar Hill and Balmuildy, and also the meat of wild animals, and fish. Analysis of the sewage at Bearsden has demonstrated the variety of the diet: wheat, barley, bean, fig, dill, coriander, opium poppy (presumably used for seasoning), raspberry, bramble, wild strawberry, bilberry, celery and hazelnut. Some of these items may have been imported from countries bordering the Mediterranean. We

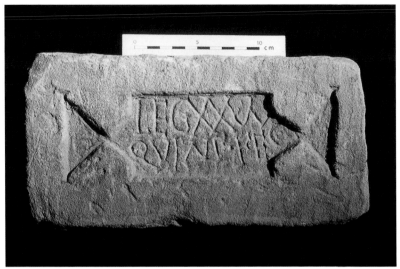

Fig. 6.9 This simple inscription found in the granary at Bearsden records building work by the Twentieth Legion.

can amplify that list with walnuts from Bar Hill and oysters, mussels and whelks there and at Mumrills.

One of the most exciting discoveries at Bearsden arose from the biochemical analysis of the sterols surviving in the sewage. This demonstrated that the balance of the diet was mainly vegetarian. While it is clear from both literary sources and the remains of animal bones in forts that soldiers ate meat, the importance of this research was to demonstrate for the first time that this was not the main element of the diet at Bearsden. Perhaps we should not be surprised. Winter feeding was always a problem, as was the storage of meat before the invention of modern methods of refrigeration.

The Vindolanda writing tablets contain references to an enormous range of foodstuffs, some required for religious ceremonies rather than day-to-day consumption. These include wheat, barley, bread, pork, ham, deer, chickens, oysters, lentils, radishes, olives, fish sauce, apples, eggs, honey, pepper and spices.

While the name of the building, *horreum* (probably derived from *hordeum* = barley), implies that only grain was kept there, we may consider that other foodstuffs were stored in the building: there is no other known location within a fort for additional food stores. We do not know where drink was stored. Beer and wine are recorded in the Vindolanda writing tablets. Fragments of large jars or *amphorae* have been found at many forts on the Antonine Wall, some marked as containing wine. Such vessels might have contained a wide range of items such as prunes or even fish sauce!

At some stage during the life of the fort at Bar Hill, a timber granary was erected within the courtyard of the headquarters building. This is not what we would expect, but a similar situation is found at Cramond, the next fort beyond the eastern end of the Wall.

BARRACK-BLOCKS

Barrack-blocks normally contained a suite of rooms at one end for the centurion, in the case of an infantry century, or a decurion in a cavalry troop, and a number of smaller rooms ranged along the length of the building and often divided into two. Our main assumptions on the occupation of these rooms is provided by an anonymous and undated, though probably fourth-century, writer, who described the arrangements of the army on campaign when the officers and men were living in tents. The centurion had a large tent placed at one end of a row of eight tents, eight men occupying each tent. Only eight tents were provided for a century of eighty men because two tent groups were on duty at any one time and simply took over the bed spaces of those soldiers who replaced them when they came off duty. The soldiers slept in the tent, and placed their arms and equipment in the space in front of the tent. On the basis of this description, we assume that when a single room in a barrack-block is divided into two, the soldiers slept in the back room and kept their arms and equipment in the front room. On the Antonine Wall, unfortunately, we have little detailed evidence of the internal divisions of barrack-blocks and in those where evidence does survive, at Bar Hill and Bearsden, the barrack room is undivided.

A Roman fort does not contain one building which would certainly be expected in a modern military establishment, a central eating hall. Soldiers might cook their food in ovens, such as are known at Balmuildy and Duntocher, and then eat their meal either at the barrack door under the veranda or inside during inclement weather. In theory, each soldier was provided with a daily ration which he cooked himself, but it is likely that the occupants of each barrack-room pooled their food with one soldier taking on the cooking responsibilities. Various items of cooking equipment were stamped with the name of the *contubernium*, a barrack-room group, and larger items, such as quern stones and mill stones for grinding corn, with the name of the century. Part of a quern stone found at Balmuildy bears the fragmentary name KAL, and was probably the property of the century. An Egyptian papyrus records the daily ration: 3 lb of bread, 2 lb of meat, 2 pints of water and ⅛ pint of oil.

WORKSHOP

One building at Bearsden has been identified as a workshop on the basis of its plan. It consists of three ranges of rooms round a small courtyard and is a much smaller version of workshops elsewhere. Unfortunately, no objects were recovered which would verify this identification.

STABLES AND STOREHOUSES

Cavalry are known to have been stationed in Antonine Wall forts therefore stables might be expected. On Hadrian's Wall some buildings have been found to serve a dual purpose, with horses stabled in the front room and soldiers quartered in the back room of a building which otherwise in plan looks like a normal barrack.

It is sometimes not possible to determine the purpose of buildings in forts. Some anonymous buildings have been tentatively identified as storehouses and smaller buildings divided into rooms as accommodation for special groups of men. It is possible that we will never be able to identify firmly such buildings.

Fig. 6.10 The bath-house at Bearsden looking south. The bather entered from the right, leaving his clothes in the changing room. From there he progressed to the cold room where he had a choice of the sauna (the room to this side of the cold room), or the steam range (to the left); beyond the cold room lay the apsidal cold bath. Top left, outside the bath-house, lay the latrine.

BATH-HOUSES AND LATRINES

Each fort, no matter how small, was provided with a bath-house and a latrine. The bath-house usually contained rooms offering two types of bathing, the steam Turkish bath and the sauna. The steam range sometimes had a hot bath, and the building might also have been provided with a cold bath. These facilities were for the use of all the soldiers in the fort, though we do not know how often they were used.

A latrine was often associated with a bath-house. Sometimes it was placed within it, elsewhere it lay in a separate building. This was a communal latrine, capable of holding several soldiers at a time: it can be calculated that the latrine at Bearsden provided sufficient

Fig. 6.11 Artist's impression of the latrine at Bearsden. Drawn by Michael J. Moore.

space for nine soldiers to use the building at once. The sewage from this latrine drained into the fort ditches, passing along a culvert under the rampart. By the time the fort was abandoned, the outer annexe ditch was about half-full of rotting sewage, though the fact that this was covered in water meant that it would not smell. The sewage also contained fragments of moss, probably used by the soldiers to clean themselves. Parasites demonstrated that the soldiers were infested with both whipworm and roundworm.

Another building not yet identified in any fort on the Antonine Wall is the hospital. There may have been such a building in each fort, or at least each larger fort, but there is insufficient evidence to confirm this.

Fig. 6.12 A gaming board found in the bath-house at Bearsden.

Fig. 6.13 The head of the goddess Fortuna found in the bath-house at Bearsden.

Fig. 6.14 Fig seeds found in the sewage at Bearsden fort. Presumably the figs were imported from the Continent.

ANNEXES

There has been relatively little excavation in annexes. Several contained bath-houses, but otherwise no major buildings have been found. At Mumrills timber buildings were located, and evidence for industrial activity. Three sculptured stones and part of an altar were recovered from the annexe at Balmuildy and indicate the existence of a shrine. Possible timber buildings were planned at Cadder to the east of the fort in an area presumed to lie in the annexe. The annexe at Camelon, just to the north of the Wall, contained timber buildings of a non-military nature.

THE FORT AS HOME

The fort was the base of the soldier. He was reasonably well paid, certainly by local standards. The pay was issued three times a year at special parades. When he joined the army, he had to buy his own weapons and pay for a share of the tent used on campaigns (the money could be regained on retirement, or by his heir if he died earlier). Money was thereafter deducted from his pay to cover food and bedding, for the camp dinner at Saturnalia (now Christmas) and the burial club. The remaining money was retained in his savings account managed by the standard bearer of his century or troop.

One of the pay parades was at the beginning of the year. Then occurred another important ceremony. On 3 January, the soldier's regiment assembled to renew its oath of allegiance to the emperor and make vows to Jupiter for the welfare of the emperor and for the eternity of the empire. The anniversary of the emperor's accession – 10 July in the case of Antoninus – would have been marked in a similar way, with prayers to the gods, and administration of the oath of allegiance to soldiers and civilians. Other anniversaries of members of the imperial family, past as well as present, were celebrated during the rest of the year. Indeed the accession day and birthday of Antoninus are known to have been commemorated well into the third century and presumably even longer. By the 200s, the first half of the year contained twenty-six such events, helping to relieve the soldier from the tedium of military life.

One duty, undoubtedly, was the maintenance of the forts and their buildings. Excavation has demonstrated that many buildings were amended and repaired, often more than once. Some of the rebuilding noted above and possibly resulting from the changes in plan during the building of the Wall may alternatively relate to care and maintenance. At Bearsden, for example, while the realignment of the bath-house can probably be associated with the decision to divide the fort into a fort and annexe, the two later phases in the building are minor amendments reflecting the change of use of one room. Soldiers at Vindolanda are recorded building a bath-house and a hospital, while amongst the raw materials listed are stones, rubble, lime, clay, lead and timber.

Each soldier would have had to undertake general fatigues, including guard duty. Guards were posted each day at the fort gates, at main road junctions within the fort, at the headquarters building, commanding officer's house and the granary. The soldiers also had to undertake duties such as cleaning the streets or the officers' uniforms and unspecified tasks at the bath-house. Many sought to escape these chores. One way was to apply for a post on the commanding officer's staff, as a clerk for example, or learn a trade. Each regiment on the Wall would have included within its ranks a variety of specialised posts: musicians for sounding the watch or signals in battle,

Fig. 6.15 The building of a fort as shown on Trajan's Column. In the foreground soldiers dig ditches; beside them lie turves ready for use in the rampart. In the gateway, a soldier relieves a comrade of a turf block. To the left, carpenters are at work. The soldiers work in armour, with their helmets and shields close by.

surveyors, guardsmen, grooms, and a doctor. Obtaining one of these posts released the soldier from ordinary fatigues. Julius Apollinarius, who was appointed to the staff of the legionary commander in Arabia in 107, wrote home triumphantly to say that he had escaped the drudgery of cutting stones all day. Other soldiers might have looked to more immediate matters, the provision of food for the regiment. There are references in the Vindolanda writing tables to the ox herds at the wood, Candidus in charge of the pigs, and the brewer.

It was not normally possible to attain one of these coveted posts with fewer than three or four years of service. One advantage is that they placed the soldier on the first rung of a promotion ladder which might lead all the way up to centurion or decurion. The *immunis*, that is the soldier rendered immune from fatigues, would next seek a promoted post, perhaps as *tesserarius*, the third in command of a century, or as *custos armorum*, who looked after the arms. These were the first of three posts immediately below centurion; the other two were *optio*, second-in-command of a century, and *signifer*, standard-bearer. This was the standard-bearer in a century; there were also regimental standard-bearers. The lucky or gifted man could then hope for promotion to centurion: if he was lucky this might occur after a minimum of about fourteen years of service. Once he had reached that position, the rules governing retirement after twenty-five or twenty-six years were waived, and he could stay on, almost as long as he liked: one centurion is recorded as having fifty-eight years of service. The centurion could also contract a marriage according to Roman law, a social act forbidden to the ordinary soldier. Soldiers, however, appear to have married according to local law or custom. This was recognised retrospectively by the state for on retirement the auxiliary soldier was not only granted citizenship but also the right to marry according to Roman law either his present or a future wife. Until the time of Antoninus, any existing children were granted citizenship, but that was changed in about 140 and thereafter existing children were excluded from this grant.

In the Roman world it was natural to ask for an appointment. Julius Apollinaris asked the governor. Pliny's letters contain many requests for favours for his friends, and the Vindolanda writing tablets include such requests. One other item which we take as normal also had to be requested, leave. In the early empire, this was at the discretion of centurions who expected payment for the privilege of granting leave. This caused great resentment until the emperor changed the system, compensating the centurions for their loss of earnings. The Vindolanda writing tablets, among many other military documents, demonstrate that the soldier had to petition for leave.

The soldier might escape military life through ill health. The strength report found at Vindolanda records that fifteen soldiers were sick, six wounded, and fifteen suffering from eye infections. He certainly tried to improve his daily life through the procuring of gifts from relatives. Letters from soldiers to their families, or *vice versa*, refer to weapons, socks, sandals, underpants and other items of clothing, and a wide variety of food, including bread, cake, cabbages, fish and oysters!

What the soldiers were not given, they might take. Complaints exist from elsewhere in the empire of soldiers stealing animals, demanding hospitality and indulging in extortion. A normal account of an agent lists the cost of bribes to soldiers.

THE FORT AS BASE

While the fort was home to the soldier, he would have spent a lot of time away from it. Simply living required him to travel. Soldiers escorted food and other supplies; perhaps they bought them as well. This could be troublesome. One man at Vindolanda grumbled about the state of the road to Catterick in the winter.

He would have been required to participate in regular training, which might take him away from base. The abandoned hill fort at Burnswark in Annandale appears to have been used as a training area for soldiers based in north Britain. Scouting and patrolling north of the Wall might have numbered amongst his duties. Some men might have had to go down to London to serve in the governor's bodyguard for a time.

The Roman state did not possess a police force and duties that we expect a civilian force to undertake fell to the army. Chasing brigands, pursuing criminals, escorting prisoners, or travellers or merchants from outside the empire were all tasks for the army. The commanding officers acted as local magistrates, and it was their soldiers who had to enforce their will. Normal peacekeeping duties might have included supervising the local market and collecting customs dues.

It is perhaps not surprising that the soldier sought help. Soldiers owned slaves, but what they were allowed to do on behalf of the soldier is not known. The place for relaxation was the civil settlement outside the fort gate.

CHAPTER VII

LIFE ON THE EDGE

... as far as the eye can stretch,
houses, temples, shops and theatres,
barracks and granaries ...

RUDYARD KIPLING,
Puck of Pook's Hill (London 1927), 173

Kipling was, of course, describing Hadrian's Wall, and a mythical Hadrian's Wall at that. One of the disappointments of excavation on the Antonine Wall is the lack of evidence found for civil settlements. There has been a conscious attempt over many years to find buildings outside forts, but with little success. The main evidence for civilians on the Wall therefore is provided by inscriptions.

PEOPLE

Inscriptions provide the names of some civilians on the frontier. Salmanes buried his 15-year-old son of the same name at Shirva between Bar Hill and Auchendavy. His name betrays an eastern origin, perhaps connected to the presence of a cohort originally raised in Syria in the adjacent fort. Verecunda was buried in the same cemetery, but her name is too common to be localised. Vibia Pacata accompanied her husband to his posting at Westerwood. Here she dedicated an altar to the nymphs of the forest and the spirits of the crossroads. There is a hint in her name and the dedications of a link either to central Europe or to Africa. This, however, is the full tally of civilians named on inscriptions. Other names appear on pottery vessels, such as Materna whose name is scratched on a samian pot found at Mumrills, while Targarus scratched his on a tile.

Places

In the face of the paucity of epigraphic evidence, why do we presume that there were civil settlements outside the Wall forts? Mainly because any army, and certainly a relatively well-paid army like the Roman force, attracted men and women eager to relieve it of money, secondly because most forts across the empire have been found to have civil settlements outside their walls, sometimes of considerable size, and thirdly because some evidence for civilians has been found on the Wall.

Literary sources show that the Roman army on campaign had camp followers. These had to stay outside the camp, unless there was a serious situation when they were allowed inside. As the army acquired a permanent base, the camp followers would presumably settle down outside the new fort. When the regiment moved on, it might be expected that the civilians moved with the soldiers. On the way, over the years, we may assume that this community acquired new members. What is difficult to know is whether any of the people from the local farms came to settle in the civil settlements outside the forts of north Britain. There is very little indication of any contact between the urban and rural worlds of the northern frontier. Few artefacts have been found on native farms, suggesting that even if the country folk came into the civil settlements, they did not return with many Roman goods, nor did their sons and daughters send home souvenirs relating to their new lives. One site south of the Forth stands out, Traprain Law in East Lothian. This has produced a wide range of artefacts, including luxury items as well as pottery, and moulds indicating the manufacture of metal objects. Traprain Law would appear to have been a major local centre with strong contacts with the Roman distribution network.

One of the most important pieces of evidence for the existence of civilians on the Antonine Wall was found by chance in 1956. It was an inscription discovered during ploughing about 150 m (450 ft) east of the fort at Carriden at the east end of the Wall. The altar is dedicated to Jupiter Best and Greatest by Aelius Mansuetus on behalf of the villagers settled at Fort Velunia (or Veluniate). These villagers clearly formed a self-governing community outside the fort. The dedication to Jupiter suggests that the dedication occurred either on 3 January or on 10 July, the anniversary of the emperor's accession. In 112, Pliny, governor of Bithynia and Pontus in Asia Minor, wrote to the Emperor Trajan reporting the ceremony to commemorate the emperor's accession and stated that the provincials were eager to take the oath of allegiance as proof of their loyalty: perhaps the altar found at Carriden was a similar proof of the loyalty of the civilian community living here.

The granting of self-governing rights to civilian communities in the frontier region is not unusual – some are known along the line of Hadrian's Wall, for example. The only surprise in this instance is that such a community should have existed during the relatively brief life of the Antonine Wall. However, bearing in mind that the community had probably simply moved north from the regiment's previous station, the arrangement is not so surprising; perhaps the administrative framework was simply moved too.

Only fragmentary traces of buildings have come to light in civil settlements. At Mumrills a line of post-holes, partly overlain by clay and cobble pads 11.6 m (38 ft) long and perhaps intended to support buildings, was found to the east of the fort in 1937. Smaller post-holes, pits, a kiln and a hearth and a gully have also been recorded, together with an altar to the Mother Goddesses. Other post-holes located in the enclosure to the east of the fort in 1958–60 may also relate to the civil settlement. West of the fort, a statuette of Hercules was recovered in 1992.

At Bearsden a single length of clay and cobble foundation was recorded west of the fort. At one end of it a stone contained a pivot hole, suggesting the existence of a doorway: presumably the rest of the building was of timber. Gullies were recorded west of the fort at Westerwood in 1987 to the south of the Military Way, together with post-holes, but no pattern was discernible. Ditches were also recorded in areas excavated in the 1970s to the south-west and to the east of the fort on Croy Hill. Pottery and artefacts were also recovered, but no buildings, though a pottery kiln was located. In 1913 an altar was found south of the fort during quarrying.

Stray altars may indicate the location of civil settlements at other sites, such as that to Victory found in 1843 200–300 m (200–300 yards) south of the fort at Rough Castle. Two altars have been found to the west of Castlecary fort, one recording the erection of a shrine. A single altar was found to the east of Bar Hill and close to the Military Way. Five altars were found in a pit a short distance beyond the south-west corner of Auchendavy fort in 1771 during the cutting of the Forth–Clyde Canal. An altar ploughed up to the east of Castlehill in 1826, dedicated to the Goddesses of the Parade-ground, may relate to a military rather than a civilian activity.

Other forms of evidence can be equally useful. Many pottery kilns must have existed along the line of the Wall for locally made pots have been recognised at several forts. One enterprising potter, Sarrius by name, appears to have opened a workshop, probably at Bearsden where many of his wares have been found. His first workshop was near Leicester; he later established a second at Rossington Bridge near Doncaster. When the army moved north, he apparently saw a business opportunity and opened a third. He is unlikely to have moved himself, but probably sent his workmen north as he did to Rossington Bridge.

Shops selling pottery are therefore likely to have existed. Although it has been argued that the army relied on contracts for the purchase of pottery, the distribution patterns of such items suggests the operation of something approaching free trade with individual merchants supplying local shops. Pottery was supplied to the Antonine Wall from Dorset, the Severn valley, Essex, Kent, the Midlands, south Yorkshire and north-west England, as well as northern Gaul. Merchants who traded pottery to Britain are recorded dedicating

Fig. 7.1 A mixing bowl bearing (upside-down) the name of Sarrius, the head of the firm which made it.

altars to the local goddesses at the port at the mouth of the River Rhine.

Many other goods came to the Antonine Wall to fulfil the requirements of soldiers and civilians. They came in a variety of containers. A small barrel found at Bar Hill was scored with the name Ianuarius, though whether he was the maker or owner of the barrel is not known. Other commodities were carried in large wine jars or *amphorae*, as we have seen.

One building has been found beside the Antonine Wall, but not near a fort. In 1980 part of a building heated by a hypocaust (underfloor heating system) was discovered and excavated immediately south of the rampart beside the West Burn at the west end of Callendar Park, Falkirk. Only one room was examined, though it was served by two hypocausts: a courtyard lay to the south. The location of the building is strange, though it lies beside an apparent gap through the Wall. Eight years previously, the ditch was found to

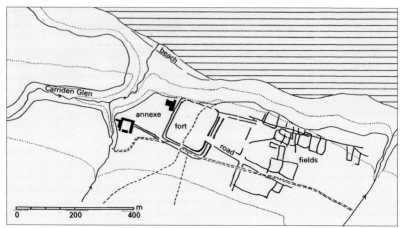

Fig. 7.2 Plan of the fort and field system at Carriden.

come to a butt-end just over 50 m (150 ft) to the west. At the east end of Callendar Park evidence for activity immediately behind the rampart, in this case a hearth with some pottery and bones, has already been noted.

The best evidence for a civil settlement outside a fort comes from Inveresk some 36 km (22 miles) to the east of the Antonine Wall. Here, excavation has revealed both timber and stone buildings, one material replacing the other, along a road leading from the east gate of the fort. A hypocausted building lies 300 m (1,000 ft) from the fort while a feature interpreted as an aqueduct leads to it. Within the settlement, pottery manufacture was certainly carried out. Beyond the buildings lay extensive field systems.

AGRICULTURE

It would be useful to be able to balance the inscription erected by the villagers of Velunia with archaeological evidence for their town or village. Alas, that has not been possible. To the east of the fort aerial photography has revealed the presence of a field system which is on the same alignment as the fort and is therefore presumed to relate to it. But no buildings have been shown to lie within this complex. The

Fig. 7.3 The field system beside the fort at Rough Castle from the air.

fields vary considerably in size, from nearly 1 ha (2.4 acres) down to small enclosures, more like horticultural plots, perhaps for the growing of vegetables.

Field systems have been recorded outside other forts along the Wall, at Rough Castle and, as we have seen, at Croy Hill and Westerwood. Those at Rough Castle are still visible and of at least two phases. A prehistoric date for them was suggested following excavation, but their proximity to the fort and the presence within them of a metalled road at right angles to the Military Way, is perhaps indicative of a Roman date. Again, they are small, more appropriate for market gardening activities.

Ditches found north-west of the fort at Auchendavy are also probably part of a field system: they certainly produced Roman pottery from their fill. There should be no surprise at this. Aqueducts crossed the land north of Hadrian's Wall to meet the needs of two forts, while civilian buildings may have lain north of the Wall at three other forts.

THE COUNTRYSIDE

While we may have problems in recognising civil settlements, we have equal difficulty in placing the Wall in its wider landscape setting. We know very little of contemporary native settlements and their occupants. It is clear that many farms must have lain along the Antonine Wall in order to produce the pasture from which the turf was cut. Further afield, two surveys of the Campsie Fells in the last sixty years have failed to provide evidence for prehistoric settlement and we must presume that they were largely devoid of farms, though, of course, they may have been used for grazing animals. The known main areas of settlement lay along the eastern edge of the hills to the north of the Antonine Wall.

The settlements included several brochs. These are round stone towers. The external perimeter contains only a single door and no windows and they give the strong impression that their builders had defence in mind. The main distribution of such structures is in north and north-west Scotland, but some are known in the south. Many have produced Roman pottery, which is still the primary dating evidence. However, that pottery ranges in date from the mid-first century to the late second century AD. Leckie, on the northern edge of the Gargurnnock Hills, has produced mid-second-century pottery. The most obvious place of derivation of that pottery is one or more of the forts of the Antonine Wall or its outpost forts. The excavator has argued that the broch was destroyed by Roman artillery, but that seems unlikely in view of the fact that it also yielded Antonine pottery.

RELIGION

As we have seen, the worship of Jupiter was an important element of the annual series of religious ceremonies celebrated by both soldiers and civilians. It is probable that each fort had a shrine to Jupiter, perhaps located in the civil settlement, where the altars dedicated to the god were placed.

Soldiers, as always, dedicated to a wider range of gods than the Roman pantheon, though on the Wall the gods of Rome predominated: Jupiter, Mars, Apollo, Mercury, Hercules, Neptune (at Castlecary, the furthest fort from the sea!), Minerva, Diana, the Nymphs, Victory, Fortuna and Silvanus. Local or British gods were sometimes identified with the Roman gods: Camulus with Mars, Magusanus with Hercules, as we have seen. The Mother Goddesses are represented just once, the Goddesses of the Parade-ground twice.

The most significant collection of altars was found in 1771 during the excavation of the Forth–Clyde Canal. Four altars dedicated by Marcus Cocceius Firmus were found in a pit together with part of a fifth, a bust and two iron hammers (see fig. 7.6). Firmus, a centurion in the Second Legion, dedicated to a wide range of gods: Jupiter Best and Greatest and Victorious Victory; Mars, Minerva, the Goddesses of the Parade-ground, Hercules, Epona and Victory; Diana and Apollo; and the Genius of the Land of Britain. Eric Birley was able to suggest, on the basis of these dedications, that

Fig. 7.4 An altar erected to Jupiter Best and Greatest by the First Cohort of Baetasians at Old Kilpatrick.

Fig. 7.5 A statue (partially restored) of Mars found in the annexe of the fort at Balmuildy.

Firmus hailed from one of the frontier provinces, probably on the Lower Danube, but had seen service in the mounted imperial bodyguard in Rome.

The historical importance of the dedication to Mercury found in the valley to the west of Castlecary has already been noted. Its other significance lies in the fact that it records the erection of a temple. Another shrine presumably existed outside the fort at Mumrills, for an altar dedicated to Hercules Magusanus by a cavalryman was found about 1.6 km (1 mile) south-east of the fort, well beyond the limit of any civil settlement. Coincidentally, Mumrills has also yielded a second item relating to Hercules, a stone statuette of the god, found 0.7 km (½ mile) west of the fort (see fig. 7.7). It has been argued that this was carried in modern times from the shrine to the south-east of the fort.

Fig. 7.6 One of the altars erected by M. Cocceius Firmus at Auchendavy.

Fig. 7.7 Statuette of Hercules found at Mumrills.

CEMETERIES

Officers, soldiers and civilians all left their ashes on the Antonine Wall. A tombstone records the death of Gaius Iulius Marcellinus, prefect of the First Cohort of Hamians, which was stationed at Bar Hill, and a second that of the soldier Nectovelius of the Second Cohort of Thracians based at Mumrills. The uninscribed tombstone of a father found at Croy shows him flanked by two soldiers, probably his sons. Rarely is it possible to locate the cemetery. The discovery of the tombstones of a soldier and of two civilians,

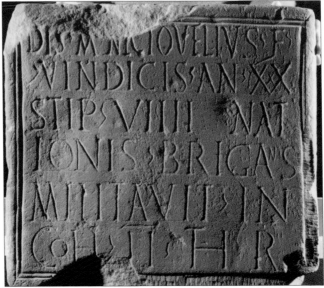

Fig. 7.8 The tombstone of Nectovelius, a Brigantian by birth, who served in the Second Thracian Cohort and was buried at Mumrills.

Fig. 7.9 The tombstone of a legionary found at Croy Hill. He is flanked by two more legionaries, perhaps his sons.

Fig. 7.10 A funeral banquet depicted on a tombstone found at Shirva.

together with two slabs depicting the funeral banquet, at Shirva between Auchendavy and Bar Hill may indicate the position of a cemetery perhaps shared by the two forts. A single cremation in a pot was found east of the fort at Croy Hill.

Immediately north of the Wall at Camelon, burials have been found both east and north-west of the fort. They include both inhumations and cremations, though all probably date to the late first century. A little further north, by Arthur's O'on, an inhumation was recorded in the nineteenth century. A stone cist contained human remains, an iron spear-head and a brooch. The brooch dates to the late first to second centuries therefore the burial may be contemporary with the Antonine Wall. Yet, the Romans normally cremated their dead at this time. Nor were weapons usually buried with soldiers; they were far too valuable to be discarded in this way. It is therefore possible that this cist and the similar one at Camelon may be of local men, though it remains possible that they were locals who had joined the Roman army.

VIII

THE FUNCTION OF
THE ANTONINE WALL

*… its real function was, to a large extent,
political and administrative.*

SIR GEORGE MACDONALD,
The Roman Wall in Scotland (Oxford 1934), 470

The Antonine Wall, as we have seen, consisted of a running barrier, a turf rampart, fronted by a ditch of varying widths, supported by defensive pits on the berm. Along the Wall were placed forts. Originally these were intended to average 13 km (8 miles) apart, but the distance was later reduced to about 3.5 km (2½ miles). The first plan seems to have included fortlets placed a little over 1 Roman mile (1.6 km) apart, and 'expansions', probably beacon platforms, and, in one area, small enclosures of uncertain purpose.

While fort walls and ramparts were provided with a protected wall-walk, no evidence survives to indicate the existence or otherwise of a walk along the top of the running barrier, though it was certainly wide enough to take one. Hadrian's Wall was similarly wide enough to have taken a wall-walk though again there is no certain evidence for one. The contemporary frontier in Germany was formed of large timbers and therefore did not possess a walkway along the top (see fig. 11.2). Nor was the Roman army equipped to fight from the tops of walls, except in emergency, and even then from fort walls not

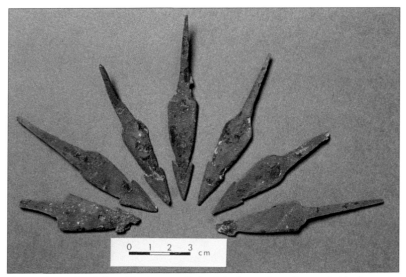

Fig. 8.1 Arrow-heads found in the west ditch of the fort at Bearsden, probably dumped there when the fort was abandoned.

barriers running for miles. It preferred to seek a military decision in the field where the soldiers' training, discipline and weapons gave them a distinct advantage.

Iron objects have not survived well on the Antonine Wall and few forts have yielded weapons. Two collections stand out. Twenty-five javelin-heads or ballista bolts were recovered from Bar Hill, most from the well, twelve arrow-heads and two spear-heads. The forty-four arrow-heads and six javelin-heads/ballista bolts found at Bears-den were also found in a rubbish deposit. In contrast, Mumrills produced eight spear-heads and the fortlet at Seabegs six javelin-heads/ballista bolts. Other such items, and ballista stones, have been found in other forts.

There was no necessity to place a walk along the top of the rampart to facilitate movement because the Antonine Wall was provided with a road, the Military Way, which appears to have been part of the original plan.

In studying the Antonine Wall, two distinctions have to be acknowledged. Firstly, that the Antonine Wall was not necessarily the boundary of the province. That may have lain elsewhere, as the

Fig. 8.2 A fort depicted on Trajan's Column. The gate and corner towers are of timber but the buildings inside the fort appear to be of stone.

existence of the outpost forts hints. The Wall was built in a particular location because that was the most convenient and useful geographical line. It may not even have marked the northernmost limit of 'Roman' settlement. Houses are known to have been built immediately north of Hadrian's Wall outside three forts, while aqueducts from north of the Wall serviced two other forts. No such evidence has been found on the Antonine Wall, though a probable field system of Roman date has been recorded north-west of Auchendavy. It would certainly come as no surprise if more evidence was found for such Roman activity in the northern lea of the Wall.

The second distinction that has to be drawn is between the linear barrier and the army bases placed on it. The purpose of the linear barrier was frontier control, whereas the primary function of the soldiers in the forts was the defence of the province. The running barrier was not defensive in its own right. It was certainly well protected, being provided with a ditch and obstacles on the berm, but there were not sufficient soldiers in the army of Britain to man it as a fighting platform.

The Antonine Wall in general followed a good line, utilising ground which gave the advantage to the Romans, though that was not always the case. East of Mumrills, the Wall took the direct line across the valley rather than swinging southwards and using the higher ground occupied by modern Polmont. On Croy Hill, the Wall also took the direct line here, ignoring the edge of the escarpment to the north (see fig. 8.3). At its western end the land rose up immediately from the Wall to the Kilpatrick Hills to the north, thereby appearing to place the Wall in a poor defensive position; presumably in this case it was regarded more important to control a particular fording point rather than take the most favourable defensive position.

In fact, the Antonine Wall was no more military in purpose than was the Berlin Wall. The function of that barrier was to prevent people leaving East Germany: in effect, its purpose was frontier control. In the event of an attack, in either direction, the existence of the Berlin Wall would not have slowed up the advance: it would simply have been blasted away.

The troops who would have created that attack force were not based on the frontier but some distance to the rear. The only difference between the defence of Western Europe in the late twentieth century and the province of Britain in the mid-second century is that many soldiers were actually in the front line, being stationed in the forts on the Antonine Wall. It is therefore more difficult to see the distinction between the two purposes as the physical manifestations of each are so intertwined on the ground. However, the protection afforded to individual forts helps to emphasise that they were seen as separate identities with their own defensive requirements.

Most of the forts had three ditches instead of the more usual two. Sometimes the arrangements could be quite elaborate. At Rough Castle, the rampart is 6 m (20 ft) wide, with a stone foundation, with an extra ditch beside the stream, possibly to give protection on a vulnerable side, and defensive pits to the north of the ditch.

The defences of these forts then, and not the Antonine Wall's rampart and ditch, protected the soldiers based on the Wall. They, in turn, protected the province. It is perhaps within that framework

Fig. 8.3 The Antonine Wall crossing Croy Hill looking east.

Fig. 8.4 The western defences of the fort at Rough Castle sitting above the
Rowan Tree Burn.

that we should see the purpose of the 'expansions'/beacon-platforms:
they provided communication with other units, the outpost forts to
the north, and the first fort on the westerly route south.

While there were two functions, both were carried out by the
army, and presumably the same soldiers. How did the army
undertake its other role of frontier control? Although we have no
evidence from Britain, regulations governing the movement of people
into the Roman empire are known on other frontiers. Writing in the
year 98, Tacitus recorded that in Germany the Tencteri complained
that they could only enter the empire if they were unarmed, under
guard and after paying a fee, and, while the Hermunduri had the
privilege of being allowed to trade within the province without
guards, others could only trade on the frontier. It would have been
convenient to collect such fees – and customs-dues – at fort and
fortlet gates, though we know little of trade between the empire and
its northern neighbours in Britain and nothing of trade routes. A
distinct problem requiring further investigation is the lack of

causeways over the ditch at fortlets. How did the Wall actually work? Is it possible that there were causeways originally and they were removed when the additional forts were placed on the Wall and the purpose of the fortlets changed? However, not all forts had causeways in front of their north gates.

There are few references to the general purpose of Roman frontiers. Inscriptions from Lower Pannonia (modern Hungary) during the reign of the Emperor Commodus (180–92), two generations after the building of the Antonine Wall, record the construction of towers and forts along the Danube 'to prevent the secret crossings of petty raiders', another purpose of Roman frontiers. An anonymous biographer writing more than two centuries after the construction of Hadrian's Wall stated that 'Hadrian was the first to build a Wall, 80 miles [130 km] long, to separate the Romans from the barbarians'. The emphasis here is on separation.

How great was that separation? It may be noted that there appear to have been very few bridges over either the Rhine or the

Fig. 8.5 The defensive pits known today as *lilia* to the north of the fort at Rough Castle.

Fig. 8.6 This scene on Trajan's Column shows pits containing stakes in front of a fort gate. The heads of defeated enemies are displayed on the fort rampart.

Danube. In the early fourth century when we know some bridges were constructed, they were strongly protected on the non-Roman side by a bridgehead fort. Until that time, the Romans do not appear to have been concerned to make communication with the empire and its neighbours easy.

Recent work in western Europe has led to the suggestion that Roman frontiers were usually closed and trade with the peoples beyond not permitted. Roman artefacts beyond the frontier date to times when the frontier was open because Roman armies were operating beyond it. In Central Europe, Roman ideas certainly percolated through the frontier for some of the people to the north built houses in the Roman style, a practice which has not yet been recognised in the Britain north of the Roman frontiers. Certainly Roman artefacts are found north of the Antonine Wall, but they are not always conducive to close dating and, as that frontier had such a brief life, it is not possible to identify which, if any, of these artefacts might have passed through it.

The frontier might also have been open in the other direction. There is evidence from other provinces, not always very clear, for supplies being obtained from outside the empire. For example, a wax tablet found north of the Rhine in Friesland in modern Holland relates to the purchase of cattle and is witnessed by two centurions.

The Romans also had treaties with some of the tribes beyond the Wall. In describing the events of 197, Cassius Dio states, 'the Caledonians instead of honouring their promises had prepared to assist the Maeatae, and Severus at that time was concentrating on the Parthian war; so Lupus had no choice but to buy peace from the Maeatae for a considerable sum of money, recovering a few captives'. The Romans not only had treaties with the Caledonians and the Maeatae, but they were prepared to support their position financially.

Again, we have no knowledge, otherwise, of the contents of such treaties in Britain, but shortly after the abandonment of the Antonine Wall, the Emperor Marcus Aurelius made peace with various states beyond the Danube. Their people were not allowed to dwell within a specified distance of the Roman frontier – 8 km (5 miles) in one case, 16 km (10 miles) in another – though this was later relaxed in the case of the Iazyges who were merely forbidden to use their own boats on the Danube and obliged to keep off the islands in the river. The emperor defined the places and days for trading, and hostages were exchanged. Recruits had to be provided for the Roman army. There are also many examples of the Romans imposing a king on a neighbouring state, as we saw in the first chapter, or deposing one who was not friendly towards them. The Romans saw no problems in interfering in the internal affairs of neighbouring states if it aided their own security.

The Romans might even maintain a military presence in a neighbouring state. A regiment was placed at the Armenian capital at times, even when this was notionally an independent state. At least two outposts were held beyond the Danube in Wallachia in the second century. Scouts were also employed. A classic description of the duties of the scouts on the northern British frontier is provided 200 years after the occupation of the Antonine Wall: 'their official duty was to range backwards and forwards over long distances with information for our generals about disturbances among neighbouring nations'. There is no reason to doubt that scouts were used to undertake the same activities to the north of the Antonine Wall.

Through treaties, diplomacy, scouting, patrolling and, when necessary, fighting, the Romans sought to control affairs beyond the frontier. When fighting did occur, it is not easy to know how the Romans reacted to an attack on them. A Roman advance was led or directed by the governor Agricola in the first century, Lollius Urbicus in the second. Sometimes the emperor took charge. This was not necessarily anything to do with the seriousness of the situation, but rather personal inclination: as Herodian remarked, Severus liked fighting. The Roman reaction to an emergency is more difficult to determine. About 180, 'the tribes in the island crossed the wall that separated them from the Roman legions, did a great deal of damage, and cut down a general and his troops'. In 367 Britain was attacked from all sides with one general killed and another circumvented. In both cases, generals were in the field at the head of the armies. But what happened in the event of a sudden attack, when Roman surveillance procedures broke down? No overall commanding officer for the Wall is known. Within the Roman army there was no mechanism known to us for one officer to assume command over others of equal rank, either on the basis of the seniority of his own commission or that of his unit, except by a specially created and temporary appointment. The only officers senior to the tribunes and prefects on the Wall were the legionary legates further south at York and at Chester. We can only assume that the pragmatic Romans would have had a procedure whereby it was accepted that one officer outranked another and took charge in such circumstances until and if the legionary legate arrived.

That assumption, however, might be wrong. There are many references to the Romans taking their time to respond to an emergency. They sought to create the appropriate task force to deal with the invasion or rebellion and appoint the best commander. In 132, Hadrian reacted to the news of a revolt in Judaea by choosing Julius Severus whom he regarded as the best man for the job; it was just unfortunate that Severus was governor of Britain at the other

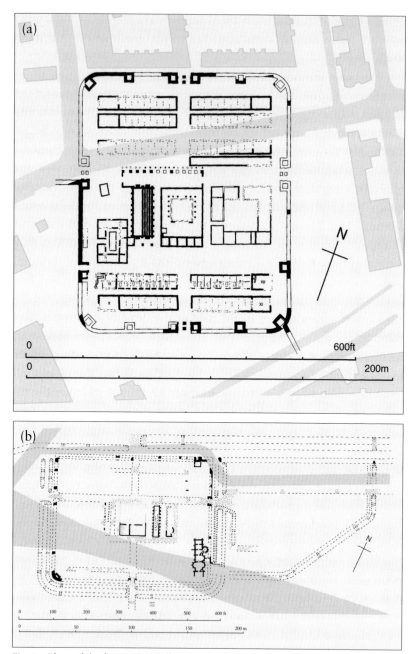

Fig. 8.7 Plans of the forts at (a) Wallsend on Hadrian's Wall and (b) Castlecary on the Antonine Wall.

end of the empire. It is possible that there were occasions when an invasion force in Britain was left to wreak havoc until the Roman army had assembled a sufficiently strong force under the right general before it responded.

The Antonine Wall sits securely within the wider framework of Roman frontiers. While we have no specific literary or documentary statement about its function, we can determine its purpose and how it was intended to work from the examination of Roman frontiers and the documents relating to them. These also demonstrate the position of the Antonine Wall in the development of Roman frontiers.

THE DEVELOPMENT OF THE FRONTIER

Hadrian was the first to order the construction of linear barriers – in Britain and in Germany – and in so doing he was making a definitive statement. He was declaring that the empire should stop expanding, should stay within its established limits. His frontier adopted types of installations long used by the army, fortlets and towers, and even ramparts and walls were part of siege-craft: the new distinctive contribution was to incorporate them into a linear barrier to create a tight system of frontier control. The Antonine Wall was a new version of Hadrian's Wall, but moving a step forward in the development of frontiers.

The use of different construction materials is not so important, and in any case, 48 km (30 miles) of Hadrian's Wall was originally built of turf. There are perhaps two significant differences. On Hadrian's Wall, the forts were all free-standing enclosures, merely placed on the Wall for convenience. Each appears to have been built for a single regiment and, if the presence of the Wall was erased from a plan, each could be seen to stand alone. On the Antonine Wall, however, the forts are closely related to the rampart. With two exceptions, they all face north, are attached to the rear of the rampart, and give the appearance of being more integrated with the whole frontier complex. This is emphasised by the construction of a

Fig. 8.8 The junction between the annexe wall (left) and fort wall at Osterburken.

road along the Wall from the very beginning whereas the road on Hadrian's Wall was an afterthought.

The other important difference lies with the smallest structures on the Wall. Although no towers are known on the Antonine Wall, there are 'expansions'/beacon-platforms and small enclosures, the latter even closer together than the turrets on Hadrian's Wall, though both occur in restricted locations.

The Antonine Wall, in fact, marked the furthest swing of the pendulum in the development of Roman frontiers. When it was abandoned and the army withdrew to Hadrian's Wall, that frontier was brought back into commission as before. There was no attempt to increase the number of forts, for example, to bring them into line with the density attained on the Antonine Wall. When changes did occur, they seemed to relate more to the local circumstances – the abandonment of turrets in the crags, for example, and the narrowing of milecastle gates – than a master plan for the frontiers.

It is instructive to compare the Antonine Wall not only to Hadrian's Wall but to the Outer Limes in Germany built nearly twenty years later. Unlike on both Hadrian's Wall and the Antonine Wall, the forts were not placed on the frontier line itself, but lay a little behind it. They were about 13 km (8 miles) apart. This was the same spacing as the forts on the earlier German frontier, 30 km (18 miles) to the west. There was no attempt to increase the density of forts as occurred on the Antonine Wall, while there was no pattern to the fortlets which were few; towers were, however, provided. At some sites there were two forts. At Osterburken, 32 km (20 miles) from the northern terminus of the frontier, there was a cohort in the fort and a *numerus* in the annexe. Twenty-six kilometres (16 miles) south lies Ohringen where there were two forts, one occupied by a cohort and the other by a *numerus*. At the southern end of the *limes* was Welzheim. Here was a cavalry regiment and, in a different fort 500 m (1,500 ft) away, a *numerus*. Dietwulf Baatz has argued that the purpose of locating two regiments together was to allow one unit from each double site to be taken off routine duties in an emergency in order to form a mobile task force without reducing the watch over the frontier.

A similar arrangement cannot be recognised on the Antonine Wall. There are no examples of double forts, though in a couple of cases the fort was too small to hold the unit attested there. In the third century, some forts on Hadrian's Wall contained additional units which may indicate a similar arrangement to the Outer Limes in Germany, while several cavalry units appear to have been placed on or around the main roads to the north.

The Antonine Wall, therefore, stands as a unique testimony to a relatively short-lived Roman military phenomenon, the frontier, and at the same time was the most developed form of that particular military installation.

CHAPTER IX

THE END OF THE ANTONINE WALL

*I can detect no trace of Roman garrisons on the wall,
or of any general occupation of Scotland by Romans,
later than the reign of Marcus Aurelius.*

F. HAVERFIELD,
in *The Antonine Wall* (Glasgow 1899), 157

DATE OF ABANDONMENT

Precisely when the Romans abandoned the Antonine Wall has long
vexed scholars. Just over 100 years ago, the eminent ancient
historian Francis Haverfield set down all the available evidence and
his resulting conclusion. The evidence cited by Haverfield was as
follows:

- no literary reference refers to the abandonment of the Antonine
  Wall or indeed any later activity on it;

- the inscriptions belong to the reign of Antoninus Pius;

- the main coins are of Domitian, Trajan, Hadrian and Antoninus
  Pius. Marcus Aurelius, Commodus and later emperors are
  almost unrepresented.

Fig. 9.1 North Britain at the time of the Emperor Septimius Severus.

LITERARY EVIDENCE

These conclusions remain true today. No new literary evidence has come to light. The biographer of Marcus Aurelius recorded that at the beginning of his reign in 161 'war was imminent in Britain and the emperor sent Calpurnius Agricola against the Britons'. The nature and location of the warfare is not otherwise attested, though it is assumed that it was on the northern frontier. The same biographer remarked that warfare was again imminent ten years later. In 175, 5,500 Sarmatians were sent to join the army of Britain, but that may have been simply to remove them as far as possible from their homeland on the middle Danube.

The next reference to warfare in Britain is even more frustrating. About 180, states Cassius Dio, 'the tribes in the island crossed the wall that separated them from the Roman legions, did a great deal of damage, and cut down a general and his troops; Commodus in alarm sent Ulpius Marcellus against them.' Later Dio commented that 'the Maeatae live by the wall which divides the country into two halves'.

At the time – and these were contemporary events to Dio – his readers would have known which wall he was writing about. Today, our interpretation of the first passage depends upon which wall we believe was occupied at the time. Since we believe that the Antonine Wall had been abandoned by 180, our presumption is that the reference was to Hadrian's Wall. So far as the second passage is concerned, it would help if we knew where the Maeatae lived. The best we can do is to point to two place-names, Dumyat and Myot Hill, both in the area of Stirling, that is to the north of the Antonine Wall, and accept the view of philologists that these may commemorate the Maeatae. If this is correct, it is likely that the place-names lay on one of the borders of the Maeatae, but which is another matter. Since there is evidence that a different people – the Goddodin – occupied Lothian to the east of Dumyat and Myot Hill, perhaps these two places lay on the southern march of the state.

INSCRIPTIONS

No inscriptions of an emperor later than Antoninus have been found on the Antonine Wall during the last hundred years. There has, however, been an attempt to date one inscription to after the reign of Antoninus. An altar to Mercury found a little to the west of the fort at Castlecary records that soldiers of the Sixth Legion, citizens of Italy and Noricum, erected a shrine and statuette. The question is: considering that the British legions recruited primarily from the north-west provinces of the empire, how did soldiers from Italy and Noricum (modern Austria) come to be among their number? John Mann argued that the most obvious occasion would be as a result of the raising of legion II Italica in 165 and its subsequent sojourn in

Fig. 9.2 The altar to Mercury erected at Castlecary by soldiers from Italy and Noricum.

Noricum. Thus, he suggested, the inscription had to date to between 165 and 190 and probably after about 175 to allow sufficient time for Noricans to have entered the legion in sufficient numbers for them to be recognised separately on the inscription. At some stage this group of soldiers had then been transferred to Britain. An appropriate occasion would possibly have been in the early 180s in order to help in the war conducted by Ulpius Marcellus. This would happily fit in with the close of hostilities on the Danube in 180. A date of 180–90 for continuing occupation of a fort on the Antonine Wall certainly flies in the face of all the other evidence. Interestingly, if any fort on the Antonine Wall might be chosen for late occupation, it is Castlecary. It has produced the latest pottery of any fort on the isthmus in both the late first century and the mid-second century and it is the only fort on the Wall with evidence for not one but two 1,000-strong infantry units. The location of Castlecary may be of relevance. It lies in an important position on the watershed between the Forth and Clyde river basins.

John Mann's argument is sound, based upon an empire-wide knowledge of the way the Roman state operated. It is, however, a unique piece of evidence and additional corroboration for such a late date for activity on the Wall would be welcome.

COINS

Haverfield's final category of evidence was coins. Four coins found on the Antonine Wall date to later than the reign of Antoninus. The latest coin found during an excavation is a fairly worn *denarius* of the Empress Lucilla, wife of Lucius Verus, and dates to 164–9. The latest coin from the Antonine Wall is a fairly worn one of Marcus Aurelius dating to 174, a stray find found in the area of the annexe at Mumrills. A coin of the same date from Camelon is also probably a stray find. One coin of Commodus was reputedly found at Kirkintilloch and possibly another at Bar Hill. These coins, however, may have as much relevance to the date of the end of the Antonine Wall as, say, the third-century coin of Constantine found at Bearsden.

Fig. 9.3 Samian pottery from the Antonine Wall.

POTTERY

The major change since 1899 lies in the study of Roman pottery. The northern frontier has been at the forefront of pottery studies because the construction of both Hadrian's Wall and the Antonine Wall is securely dated and offers baselines for dating pottery deposits. The dating of Roman pottery is now much more sophisticated, and therefore more helpful.

A major survey of samian pottery – a special type of red ware made in Gaul and imported into Britain – led Brian Hartley to suggest in 1972 that the Antonine Wall was abandoned about 163. In reaching this conclusion the pottery from Scotland was compared to collections from elsewhere. Within Scotland, material from military sites was compared to that from civilian settlements. A difference was noticed in that there was some samian dating to the late second century from civilian sites. It was clear that it was not that samian was not arriving in Scotland; it was simply not present on the Antonine Wall because the Wall had been abandoned.

South of the Antonine Wall, there is evidence to be taken into account. A lost inscription found between milecastle 11 and milecastle 13 on Hadrian's Wall records rebuilding work: it dates to 158. In the same year, an inscription recorded building work at the fort at Birrens in Annandale. This was erected during the governorship of Julius Verus. The only other evidence for the date of his governorship is part of a military diploma found at Ravenglass on the Cumbrian coast which shows that he was governor on 27 February 158, and therefore presumably already here the previous year. He is also attested building at the fort at Brough-on-Noe in Derbyshire.

A third inscription is more difficult to interpret. A slab found in the River Tyne at Newcastle and dating to the governorship of Verus records the movement of troops between Britain and Germany. There has been much discussion about the wording of the inscription and its interpretation. The best translation, requiring no amending of the text, is that the inscription records a detachment drawn from all three British legions being sent to the army of the two Germanies. The focal point of the action, the River Tyne, is most interesting. It suggests that the soldiers were already on the northern frontier.

There is a possible occasion for the transfer of British troops to Germany. At about this time, the governor of Upper Germany, Caius Popilius Carus Pedo, was commanding a special force made up not only of his own provincial army but also of soldiers from outside the province; it is possible that he was reacting to an unrecorded attack by the Chatti, who certainly invaded the empire in 161. Pedo's governorship dates from about 151 to 155 but it is not known whether the situation he dealt with had been resolved by then.

CONCLUSIONS

To return to the date of abandonment of the Antonine Wall. One of the other conclusions drawn by Brian Hartley from his study of the samian pottery is that there is very little overlap between the name-stamps of potters represented on the two Walls: in short, they were not held at the same time. Accordingly, when we have an inscription recording the rebuilding of Hadrian's Wall – and one of its outpost forts, Birrens, and, about the same time, one of its hinterland forts, Brough – the most straightforward conclusion is that the Antonine Wall was about to be abandoned for its southern counterpart.

A date of 158 for the start of the abandonment of the Antonine Wall would fit with most of the evidence from the Wall. One exception is the coin of Lucilla from Old Kilpatrick. Perhaps the best interpretation of this is that the process of abandonment took some years to achieve. This may be supported by inscriptions from Hadrian's Wall which record building work and other activities there after 158. Two fragmentary building inscriptions record work at Chesters under Antoninus Pius. Although traditionally dated to the beginning of his reign, they could equally well date to the end. Calpurnius Agricola, sent to govern Britain in 161, was recorded building at the strategically important fort Corbridge, probably in 163, which is very suggestive of change on the frontier. Under the same governor, work was undertaken at Vindolanda beside Hadrian's Wall and at Ribchester in Lancashire. An inscription from Great Chesters on Hadrian's Wall records work there later in the same decade. The implication of the evidence from both Walls is that the process of withdrawal from one Wall and repair and rebuilding on the other may have taken almost as long as the building of the Antonine Wall. Indeed, there can have been very few years in the late 150s when soldiers were not building or rebuilding one Wall and demolishing the other. The realisation that the building of the Antonine Wall may have taken twelve years or more allows us to view as realistic the possibility that the abandonment of that Wall may have taken as long as six years or more from the decision in or shortly before 158 to some time after 164.

A hundred years of research since Haverfield has not led archae-ologists to shift the date of the abandonment of the Antonine Wall. This is not to say that there are no dissenting voices. John Mann has pointed to the general decline in the quantity of coins minted after about 160, and that the main circulation of coins at any one time usually is of the previous emperor's reign and earlier. He also noted that Commodus was damned and his name erased from inscriptions. While he was later rehabilitated by the Emperor Septimius Severus, Commodus had not been popular in Britain and it is possible that nothing was done to restore his memory here, which might account for the gap in the record of his reign in the island.

DECISION MAKING

All our evidence is unequivocal: it was the emperor who decided where the limit of the Roman empire lay. The decision to abandon the Antonine Wall, on the basis of the material discussed above, was made by the very man who ordered its construction, Antoninus Pius. As we have already noted, he would have taken advice. One of the men to whom he turned to at this time may have been the man whom he had sent to Britain as governor in 139 and who started the construction of the Wall, Lollius Urbicus.

Urbicus was prefect of the city of Rome in the 150s. His term of office certainly lay in the 150s because he is mentioned in the writings of the Christian martyr Justin which date to this time. Clarus, prefect of the city, died in 146, and an unnamed prefect in 160. It is not impossible that Urbicus served in this post throughout these fourteen years: his biographer stated that Antoninus retained men in office for many years.

While proof is not possible to obtain, there is a strong chance that Urbicus was available to offer advice to his emperor as Antoninus contemplated new action in Britain: and who better was there to offer such advice?

There is, in fact, another candidate. Anthony Birley has drawn attention to the coincidence of the retirement of Antoninus' long-serving praetorian prefect Marcus Gavius Maximus in about 157 and the presumed date of the decision to withdraw from the Antonine Wall. He has suggested that the retirement of Maximus after an unprecedented 20-year term, during which he will have played a major part in directing imperial military affairs, may have been the impetus for a review of commitments.

We can only guess at the reasons for abandonment of the Antonine Wall. Perhaps the long-drawn-out building programme sapped morale. The stationing of legionaries at some forts on the Wall suggests that the army was being overstretched. Furthermore, the strength of the provincial army was itself undermined by the sending of troops to serve elsewhere. And if the reason for the move north had been in order to bring a new emperor military prestige, after twenty years on the throne, he no longer needed such a prop, which could now be discarded with impunity.

DATE	TROOP MOVEMENT
128/38	Detachment of Second Cohort of Tungrians in Noricum (modern Austria)
147–?153/57	Detachment of Second Cohort of Tungrians in Raetia (modern south Germany)
	The soldiers presumably moved from one province to the other without returning to Britain.
145–50	Soldiers sent from Britain to participate in the Moorish War in north Africa?
	The expeditionary force may have included part of the First Cohort of Vardullians and the First Cavalry Regiment of Asturians.
about 158	Legionaries sent from Britain to Germany.

Table 8 Troop movements in relation to Britain during the reign of Antoninus Pius

DEMOLITION

At the moment of abandonment, the Roman attitude to the Antonine Wall varied. The rampart was not demolished, the ditch was not

Fig. 9.4 The timber buildings at Bearsden, and the rampart breastwork (above), were burnt when the fort was abandoned: the debris filled the drains and hollows within the fort.

filled in, as the survival of both today in part at least demonstrates. Buildings within forts were demolished and burnt. At Bearsden, a 1.5 m (5 ft) wide strip of burnt wattles was interpreted as the breastwork thrown down from the east fort rampart and burnt *in situ*. The ramparts of the fort, however, were not levelled; they survived sufficiently high for William Roy to survey and plan them in 1755.

Inscriptions were dealt with differently. A record of the discovery in 1847 of a distance slab at Castlehill survives. It states that it was 'found in stiff clay, more than three feet [1 m] below the surface …. But it was not lying flat; it was on its edge showing that it must have been thrust into a little pit opened in the clay and afterwards covered up.' Two slabs found nearby on Hutcheson Hill in 1865 and 1969 were both lying flat, the latter face downwards in what the ploughman thought was a shallow pit. It would appear that in these cases, and presumably others, the soldiers took down and buried the records of their achievements. The relative freshness of many of the distance slabs is testimony to the fact that they were not long exposed to the elements.

Elsewhere, a fort's well was a useful repository of altars and other material. The well in the fort at Bar Hill was found on the very first day of the excavation, 20 November 1902, and emptied with great enthusiasm. It was 13 m (43 ft) deep – exactly the same dimension as Mousa Broch is high! It contained an enormous amount of material: coins; arrow-heads; broken pottery; a bag containing many iron objects including staples, hinges, split pins and nails; part of a window grille; an altar; seven bucket hoops together with the overhead gear and pulley; two fragments of an inscription and a part of a second; several column shafts and five capitals and bases from columns. It would appear that the army jettisoned in the most convenient location what it could not carry away.

Whether the army ever returned to the Antonine Wall, we cannot tell. It could be argued that the coins of Marcus and Commodus and the shrine to Mercury at Castlecary indicate that the army maintained outposts on the Antonine Wall into the later second century. We have already seen that outposts might have been maintained beyond the frontier. In the most extreme case known to me, soldiers of the Twentieth Cohort of Palmyrenes, based at Dura Europos on the Euphrates, sent soldiers to man an outpost 250 km (150 miles) away.

There is no indication that the Emperors Septimius Severus and Caracalla paid any attention to the Wall when they crossed it during their campaigns against the Caledonians and Maeatae between 208 and 210. All our sources are silent on the point. Yet, the great earthwork itself remained as a mute testimony to a time when the Antonine Wall was the north-west frontier of the Roman empire.

CHAPTER

GRIM'S DYKE

Near Elf-hill, according to tradition, Grime with
his Britons, broke through the wall; from which circumstance
it might possibly have the name of Grime's Dyke.

W. ROY,
The Military Antiquities of the Romans in North Britain
(London 1793), 161

Sometime in the Middle Ages, the Antonine Wall acquired a new name. John of Fordun, writing in the fourteenth century, stated that is was called 'Grymisdyke' because it had been destroyed by Gryme, grandfather of King Eugenius, himself a mythical figure. George Buchanan, traducer of Mary Queen of Scots and tutor to the young James VI, offered another story. Graeme was a leader of the Picts and Scots who broke down the Wall from the south so that his countrymen could invade the Roman province. The name survives today in Grahamsdyke Road and Grahamsdyke Lane in Bo'ness and Grahamsdyke Street in Laurieston. Its origin is probably more prosaic than either of our stories. It has been suggested that it derives from the Gaelic word *grym* meaning strong.

If the name Grim's Dyke has survived down to the present century, the Antonine Wall has had many different names in the meantime. To George Buchanan writing in the sixteenth century it was the *vallum Severi*, the Wall of Severus. The discovery of an inscription of Lollius Urbicus at Balmuildy in 1699 confirmed that the earthworks across the Forth–Clyde isthmus were the remains of the Wall known to have been built by the Emperor Antoninus Pius in Britain. John Horsley correctly ascribed its construction to the Emperor Antoninus Pius in his *Britannia Romana* published in 1732, but called it the Roman Wall in Scotland. William Roy in his *The Military Antiquities of the Romans in Britain*, published in 1793, offered as many as three names. On the title page appears 'The Wall of Antoninus Pius commonly called Grime's Dyke', both names being used inside. However, the heading of Chapter 4 is 'The Roman Wall in Scotland called Grime's Dyke'. Sometimes the two frontiers, the Antonine Wall and Hadrian's Wall, were differentiated as 'the barrier of the upper isthmus' and 'the barrier of the lower isthmus'. The Caledonian Wall was also occasionally used to distinguish the Antonine Wall from Hadrian's Wall, misleadingly termed the Picts Wall from the sixteenth through to the nineteenth century. Robert Stuart in his *Caledonia Romana*, published in 1852, called it the Wall of Antoninus Pius. This was amended to the Wall of Antonine in the Antonine Wall report published in 1899, but the name on the book's cover was 'The Antonine Wall'. The Society of Antiquaries of Scotland preferred the name the Antonine *vallum* in the reports on its excavations at Castlecary and Rough Castle and Sir George Macdonald entitled his magisterial survey, first published in 1911, *The Roman Wall in Scotland*, although he generally called it the Antonine Wall in the papers recording his work along its line in the *Proceedings of the Society of Antiquaries of Scotland*. Accordingly, it would appear that the honour of providing the definitive modern name for the Antonine Wall falls to the Glasgow Archaeological Society.

The first certain reference to the Antonine Wall after the end of Roman Britain was by the Venerable Bede. Writing at the twin monastery of Jarrow/Wearmouth in about 730, he stated that in the fifth century a Roman army returned to Britain to deal with an invasion of the Picts and Scots and advised the Britons to build a Wall for protection. 'The islanders built this wall as they had been instructed, but having no engineers capable of so great an undertaking, they built it of turf and not stone, so that it was of small

Fig. 10.1 The medieval motte in Peel Park, Kirkintilloch.

value. However, they built it for many miles between the two estuaries, hoping that where the sea provided no protection, they might use the rampart to preserve their borders from hostile attack. Clear traces of this wide and lofty earthwork can be seen to this day. It begins about two miles west of the monastery of Aebbercurnig [Abercorn] at a place which the Picts call Peanfahel and the English Penneltun, and runs westward to the vicinity of the city of Alcluith [Dumbarton].'

It is doubtful if Bede ever saw the Antonine Wall – the furthest north he is known to have travelled is Lindisfarne – but his testimony that it survived to his day is valuable. Indeed, the Wall survived for another 800 years and was visible to Timothy Pont who included it on his map of Scotland in the sixteenth century (see fig. 2.5). In 1755 William Roy could still map it from end to end, observe the Military Way and prepare plans of ten forts (see fig. 2.6). It was not just

villages which had obscured or destroyed the Wall, but agriculture too. Roy had such a good eye for the ground that his surmise at the location of the Wall even when nothing was visible was usually correct. The eastern end of the Wall had already been lost to knowledge, but Roy assumed that it ended at Carriden.

Up to then damage had been piecemeal. The forts certainly provided a useful source of building stone, but elsewhere the Wall was utilised in different ways. An underground passage (souterrain) using Roman stones was built within the ditch at Shirva: it may have been used for storage by the occupants of an adjacent farm. In the Middle Ages those concerned with defence erected castles on the Wall, at Inveravon, Watling Lodge, Seabegs, Kirkintilloch and Cadder; those at Inveravon, Seabegs and Kirkintilloch still survive.

Two events conspired to prevent the long-term preservation of the Antonine Wall: the Agricultural Revolution and the Industrial

Revolution. The late eighteenth century witnessed serious damage to the Roman earthworks in the face of new enclosures and improved methods of ploughing, and this continued well into the twentieth century. In the later nineteenth century, central Scotland became the scene of considerable industrial activity. One of the two forts at Camelon immediately north of the Wall succumbed to a series of iron furnaces; other furnaces were built at Bonnybridge. One reason for this activity was that the area was found to be rich in the kind of clay required to make the bricks for the furnaces. Mining extended under and around the Wall and resulted in subsidence which can still be seen at Rough Castle. Brickworks were required: one was built on the Wall to the west of Castlecary in 1886. Water was important in several industrial processes. In 1743 Arthur's O'on was demolished to provide stone for the mill dam of the Carron ironworks, while a small reservoir was created within the ditch between Westerwood and Dullatur.

Industrial workers required housing and the small towns and villages along the Wall recorded by Roy expanded accordingly. By 1910, Bo'ness had still not spread onto the ridge to the south along which the Wall ran. Laurieston remained a village while the growth of Falkirk was restricted to the east by the policies of Callendar House and to the west by those of Bantaskine House, both estates containing the visible remains of the ditch. Bonnybridge lay wholly north of the Wall, but Twechar sat astride the frontier and the long history of Kirkintilloch had led to much damage. Bearsden, clustering round the railway station, was already threatening the Wall, and Duntocher likewise, while Old Kilpatrick had rendered the western end of the Wall invisible even to Roy.

Building has continued apace. New housing of the 1960s in particular fills the whole area between the forts of Bearsden and Castlehill. Callendar Park fell prey to high-rise towers, Bantaskine to a housing estate. The unstoppable spread of Cumbernauld brings it to the southern edge of the Wall. And today's workers require places for leisure. Three golf courses and a ski slope lie on or beside the Wall. In death, too, we affect the Wall, with cemeteries at various locations along its course.

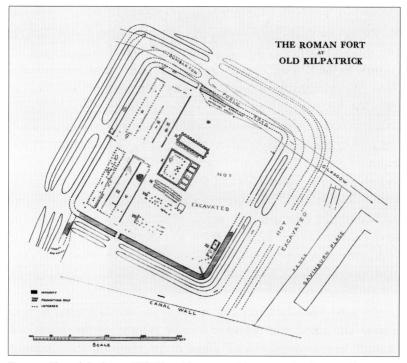

Fig. 10.2 Plan of the fort at Old Kilpatrick excavated in 1923–4 in advance of house building.

Buildings require stone, roads need an even harder stone. Thus, geology is another potent force amongst the agents of destruction. Until the twentieth century, quarries were relatively small. A quarry lay towards the west end of Bo'ness, two small sand pits are recorded on the Wall at Adamslee to the west of Kirkintilloch. In the 1930s the fort at Cadder was lost to gravel quarrying and in the 1960s part of the Wall at Wilderness Plantation. Today, further east, large quarries offer the very real possibility of leaving the Wall crossing Croy Hill on an artificial ridge.

The very location of the Antonine Wall too has been to its disadvantage. It was constructed along a convenient line. As Scotland expanded, better communication was required: the line of the Wall was often chosen. From 1768 to 1790, the Forth–Clyde Canal was cut across the isthmus. Its excavation immediately south

Fig. 10.3 Antoninus Pius depicted on the frieze in the Scottish National Portrait Gallery, Edinburgh. The frieze was created in the 1880s, just at the time that scientific archaeological research was beginning on the Antonine Wall.

of the fort at Auchendavy led to the discovery of several Roman altars. The canal was followed by the railway in the nineteenth century and motorways and other major roads in the twentieth century. Travelling from Edinburgh to Bearsden in the 1970s I crossed the Wall no less than six times.

While much of the Antonine Wall was lost because of ignorance and the lack of protection, there was also an appreciation that it was difficult – and perhaps wrong – to stop the march of progress. Excavation of the remains was normally seen as a substitute for preservation. Yet, at times there were protests, not least when Arthur's O'on was demolished in 1743; Sir John Clerk of Penicuik erected a replica over the entrance to his stables at Penicuik House.

Public knowledge of and interest in the Romans grew too. The frieze in the Scottish National Portrait Gallery, created in the 1880s, included a depiction of several Romans, including the Emperor Antoninus Pius. A stained glass window of a Roman soldier adorned Kirkintilloch Town Hall throughout most of the twentieth century. Bars along the line of the Wall commemorated its former existence, and street names perpetuated its memory. Grahamsdyke Road was supplemented by Roman Road and Antonine Court.

Fig. 10.4 (above) The coat-of-arms of Kirkintilloch includes a representation of the Roman fort known to lie under the medieval castle in Peel Park.

Fig. 10.5 (right) This stained glass window depicting a Roman soldier formerly adorned the Kirkintilloch council offices. The offices were built between 1904 and 1906; the window was removed in 1987.

Fig. 10.6 (below) The Roman Bar in Camelon.

Almost one-third of the Wall has now been obscured by post-Roman activities but the remaining parts of the monument are scheduled under the Ancient Monuments and Archaeological Areas Act 1979. Scheduling started in the 1920s, and has been reviewed thrice since, in the 1950s, 1970s and 1990s. In 1956 the National Trust for Scotland placed three sections of the Wall in state care: Watling Lodge, Rough Castle and Seabegs Wood. Further lengths have been acquired so that 10 km (6 miles) of the Wall, four forts, two bath-houses, a fortlet, three 'expansions', sections of the Military Way and several quarry pits are now in the care of Historic Scotland.

In the late 1950s, Historic Scotland's predecessor took the first steps towards protecting the environs of the Wall. Amenity zones were identified, and these were formalised in David Skinner's report, *The Countryside of the Antonine Wall*, published in 1973. Today, these amenity zones form the basis of the buffer zones around the monument which are required by UNESCO before it will consider the nomination of the Antonine Wall as a World Heritage Site. The Antonine Wall is better protected than at any stage in its past since it left the care of the Roman army: its nomination as a World Heritage Site is a logical next step for Rome's North-West Frontier.

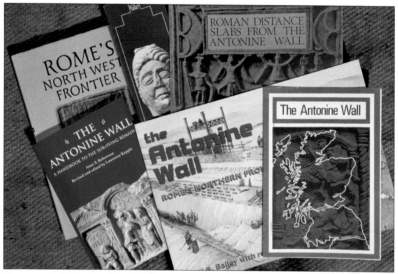

Fig. 10.7 Guide-books about the Antonine Wall.

CHAPTER XI

FINAL THOUGHTS

The Antonine Wall is Scotland's chief Roman monument.

LAWRENCE KEPPIE,
The Legacy of Rome: Scotland's Roman Remains
(Edinburgh 2004), 127

We have now reviewed the evidence for the building and history of the Antonine Wall; we have considered why it was built and also why it was abandoned. It must be emphasised that these are the views of one writer. While many are shared by other archaeologists, not all would agree with them. Most certainly my own views will change – as they have in the past – as new evidence comes to light. My own views are governed by my own prejudices. I have a particular view of the Roman army inculcated by my teachers at Durham University, and most of my work and ideas since have been within that framework. As we all know, it is difficult to think outside the box.

In writing a book such as this, then, I will naturally have stressed those fragments of evidence which better support my own views and have given less credence to those which do not. I see Roman Britain as sitting within an empire and the needs of the ruler of that empire as sometimes more influential than the local situation. To me, Roman Britain can only be explained through an understanding of the mores, aims and policies of the wider Roman empire.

Fig. 11.1 Coin of the Emperor Septimius Severus.

This was understood by Anthony Birley who first argued that we should seek the reason for the advance into Scotland within the framework of the reign of Antoninus. The emperor's problems lay at the root of the invasion and, it seems to me, this is underlined by all the available evidence: the sole acclamation of *Imperator* for any military action during his reign; the comment of Fronto about the emperor directing the invasion from the palace; the glory of the distance slabs. This event was something special, and this is emphasised, in spite of the poor sources for his reign, by the lack of comparable inscriptions on the German frontier as well as the lack of additional imperial salutations.

I have argued that at this time Antoninus Pius could have conquered the rest of the island had he been so minded, but chose not to because all he wanted was an easy victory leading to military prestige, so important in a military dictatorship. On this, I have been taken to task by Nick Hodgson who points out that the military resources of the empire were overstretched at the time. The empire was unable to bring together sufficient troops in order to deliver the knockout blow, the blow which Agricola had thought he had achieved sixty years before and Severus, too, sixty years later. There is support for this point of view. At least one British unit had sent a detachment to the continent during the reign of Antoninus; it seems probable that British troops fought in the Moorish War of the 140s; there seem to have been insufficient auxiliary regiments available in Britain to man the Antonine Wall, leading to the use of legionary detachments. The drafting of troops from so many provinces to fight in the Moorish War might be thought to support the argument that the empire's armies were overstretched, but the situation is not as simple as that. There was a relatively small military force in north Africa and any serious trouble there would have required outside help to quell in any case. Nor were these the only troop movements. During the governorship of Julius Verus, about 158, an inscription from the River Tyne at Newcastle records a detachment drawn from the three British legions being sent to reinforce the army of the two German provinces.

Part of the underlying problem here was the settlement reached by the first emperor, Augustus (31BC–AD14). The massive armies which had fought against each other during the civil wars of the first century BC had been reduced to twenty-eight legions by Augustus. There were now twice as many legions in existence than there had been in 59BC before Caesar launched the conquest of Gaul, and these were sufficient, together with the auxiliary forces, to protect the empire. New legions sometimes had to be raised if expansion of the empire was planned, while threats from outside might create severe pressures. A serious invasion in one location often required help from another province before it could be repulsed. A more serious invasion led to a more complex response. The victories by the

Dacians over the Romans in the 80s resulted in the permanent reduction in size of the army in Britain: one legion was required and, apart from a brief period, was not replaced. When necessary, whole legions were transferred from one province to another, but, as the years passed and the frontier arrangements became more fossilised, detachments rather than complete legions were sent to the trouble spot. This, though, had early roots for even when Agricola was fighting at Mons Graupius in 83, part of one of his legions was fighting on the Continent. There was also movement in the opposite direction. Under Hadrian, Titus Pontius Sabinus led an expeditionary force composed of detachments of three legions to Britain.

Nick Hodgson, therefore, has a good point, though even if Antoninus was not prepared to contemplate dealing finally with the problem of the British frontier through its total eradication, Septimius Severus was and presumably believed that he had the resources to achieve it. Furthermore, the argument that the move north was simply in order to provide Antoninus with a triumph downplays the comment of Pausanias that there was trouble on the northern frontier in Britain, or at least relegates it to a *casus belli*. However, since we do not understand Pausanias' comment, it would be dangerous to use it to support any argument.

Our understanding of the building programme for the Antonine Wall has changed considerably over recent years through the suggestions of Geoff Bailey, Nick Hodgson and Vivien Swan. Approaching the subject from different directions, their work has combined to suggest a much longer and more complex building programme than we had hitherto imagined. Each suggestion, too, is based upon evidence of different kinds or from other frontiers or provinces. Not least, these new conclusions relate to the problem of military resources. It may be too soon to determine whether these views on the length of the building programme are correct. It is impressive, however, that the new theories do not contradict each other, but rather feed off each other to create an integrated framework of activities and events. Equally significantly, they offer a serious challenge to all our previously held theories concerning the building of the Antonine Wall.

YEAR	EVENT
139	Rebuilding at Corbridge on Dere Street by Hadrian's Wall
142	Victory celebrated; Balmuildy built? Urbicus leaves Britain?
143	Wall from Castlehill to Seabegs built with primary forts, fortlets, 'expansions', small enclosures and Military Way
144	Wall from Seabegs to Bo'ness built with primary forts, fortlets, 'expansions' and Military Way
144/5	Building of secondary forts began; fortlets amended annexes started to be added to forts? Wall from Castlehill to Old Kilpatrick built?
145–50	Some troops sent to fight in Mauretania, in north Africa? Building work on Wall slowed or even ceased
147–?153/57	Detachment of Second Cohort of Tungrians in Raetia (modern south Germany) and possibly earlier in the reign in Noricum (modern Austria)
151?	Troops return to Britain from north Africa?
151+	Work recommences on the Antonine Wall
154–55	Coin issued showing *Britannia* and indicating a victory in Britain
about 155+	Annexes added (or continued to be added) to forts; Bearsden divided into fort and annexe; Duntocher fort built; Wall from Castlehill to Old Kilpatrick built (if not earlier)
about 158	Legionaries sent from Britain to Germany
158	Rebuilding on Hadrian's Wall and at Birrens
161	'War was threatening in Britain'
163	Rebuilding at Corbridge
about 163	Samian pottery indicates date of the abandonment of the Antonine Wall
164–9	Date of coin of the Empress Lucilla found in the granary at Old Kilpatrick
?180–90	Date of inscription recording the erection of a shrine at Castlecary

Table 9 Events in northern Britain relating to the Antonine Wall and its abandonment

We remain uncertain when the Wall was abandoned. John Mann placed great emphasis on the existence of an inscription on the Antonine Wall which, on the basis of empire-wide information, he believed dated to 180 to 190. This argument was so powerful to him that he continued to argue that our interpretation of the other evidence is wrong. He may be right. Explanations can be offered for the lack of coins later than the reign of Antoninus Pius on the Antonine Wall. Pottery dating is not exact. However, a crucial point for me is that Brian Hartley did not argue that there was no samian from Scotland later than about 165, but there was none from the military sites.

Even if we were to determine the exact date, the reason would probably still elude us because our literary sources are silent and archaeological evidence is not capable of providing answers to such questions. One central fact should not be forgotten: it was the emperor who decided where the boundaries of the empire should lie.

With that in mind, we can consider the occupation and abandonment of the Antonine Wall within a British context. The province was clearly problematic: or perhaps it was just the northern frontier that was problematic. Throughout the second century it was clearly a trouble spot. British regiments appear to have won battle honours during the reign of Trajan (98–117). When Hadrian succeeded, the 'Britons could not be kept under Roman control'. A centurion buried at Vindolanda about this time had been killed in warfare. Fronto remarked on the large numbers of soldiers killed in Britain during the same reign. Under Antoninus Pius, the Brigantes did something on the northern frontier according to Pausanias. At the beginning of the reign of Marcus Aurelius (161–80), 'war was threatening in Britain. Calpurnius Agricola was sent to deal with the Britons.' Under Commodus (180–92), 'the tribes in the island crossed the wall … did a great deal of damage, and cut down a general and his troops'. The new governor sent by Septimius Severus in 197, Virius Lupus, was faced with a war and had to buy peace 'for a considerable sum of money'. Ten years later, the emperors Septimius Severus and Caracalla themselves came over to campaign against the Caledonians and Maeatae.

In the face of this near continuous disruption, it is not surprising to find the best generals of the day serving in Britain. In 132, at the beginning of the Jewish War, 'Hadrian sent his best generals against the Jews. First of these was Julius Severus, who was sent from Britain where he had been governor.' Statius Priscus, governor in 162, after only about a year in office, was despatched to command the Roman forces opposed to the Parthians. Other governors had considerable military experience, either as governors of other provinces, or gained during the Jewish War: Lollius Urbicus, Julius Verus and Statius Priscus all served in that war.

Furthermore, a large army was maintained in the province, perhaps 50,000 strong. Here we must beware of circular arguments. It is often stated that the army was large because of the threat presented by the Caledonians. While the threat was certainly real, it was also the very size of the army which resulted in senior generals being sent to command it. It is also possible that the army was somewhat larger than might be expected because of the difficulties of reinforcing it.

How should we see the Antonine advance and withdrawal within this framework? If the northern frontier was volatile, could the Antonine advance merely have been an attempt to deal with it? If so, the passage in Pausanias is relevant. Even if we continue to place more weight on the arguments surrounding the necessity for Antoninus Pius to gain a military success, is it possible that the withdrawal was a different reaction to this endemic problem? Perhaps the long-drawn-out building programme had reduced the empire's leader to such desperation that he decided to abandon it altogether. Perhaps all the troop movements, which at least we can recognise if not explain, eventually produced an appreciation that the holding of the Antonine Wall was overstretching Rome's military resources and they would be better to pull back to the line of Hadrian's Wall. The retirement of the most senior army officer in the empire, the praetorian prefect Gavius Maximus, at about this time, as we have seen, may have been the occasion for reviewing frontier commitments. It is interesting – and we can say no more than that – that the abandonment of the Antonine Wall in Britain coincided with

Fig. 11.2 A reconstructed stretch of the timber palisade and stone tower on the German frontier.

the moving forward of the frontier in Germany. If there was a connection, it completely eludes us. Or was it that, faced with competing priorities and limited resources, the acquisition of more rich farmland in Germany was preferable to holding on to the hills between the Tyne–Solway isthmus and the Forth–Clyde line?

What is certain is that archaeologists and historians will continue to argue about the reasons for the northern advance and withdrawal, that new evidence will continue to be found which will alter our perceptions, and that reviewing the existing evidence will produce new ideas. The Antonine Wall may have been abandoned nearly two millennia ago, but the study of it is still very much alive.

APPENDIX I

THE REGIMENTS OF THE ANTONINE WALL

CARRIDEN
No regiment is attested here.

MUMRILLS
ala I Tungrorum
This cavalry unit was originally raised in Gallia Belgica (modern Belgium, where Tongeren retains the name) in the aftermath of the Civil War of 68/69 and sent to Britain. It served on the Danube but had returned to Britain by 98. A junior officer of the unit, Valerius Nigrinus, dedicated an altar to Hercules Magusanus at Mumrills.

cohors II Thracum
Originally raised in Thrace (modern Bulgaria). Nectovelius, a Brigantian, died at Mumrills after nine years of service. It has been suggested that the formula on his tombstone indicates a first-century date for this inscription

FALKIRK
No evidence for a unit.

ROUGH CASTLE
cohors VI Nerviorum
Raised in Gallia Belgica following the Civil War of 68/69 and sent to Britain, it is recorded at Great Chesters on Hadrian's Wall and at Bainbridge in the Pennines in the third and fourth centuries. The cohort left an inscription recording that it erected the headquarters building. For a time it was temporarily commanded by Flavius Betto, a centurion of the Twentieth Legion.

CASTLECARY

cohors I Tungrorum milliaria peditata
The unit was originally raised in modern Belgium. It was in Britain by
the late first century and based at Vindolanda. The cohort was building at
Castlecary, and may then have moved on, though equally may have stayed
as the primary garrison. In the third and fourth centuries it was based at
Housesteads.

cohors I Vardullorum milliaria peditata
Originally raised in Spain, its location in Britain is not known before it
arrived at Castlecary, where it was commanded by Trebius Verus. Verus was a
prefect and the normal title of the commander of a milliary unit was tribune:
this suggests that part of the unit was absent from its main base, possibly in
Africa. In the third century the regiment was based at High Rochester: an
inscription found at Jedburgh suggests that it operated in southern Scotland
at that time. Castlecary is too small to have held either unit at full strength.

An inscription to Fortuna in the fort bath-house dedicated by soldiers of
the Second and Sixth Legions suggests that a legionary detachment may have
been based at the fort. This is supported by the existence of two altars
dedicated by soldiers of the Sixth Legion, one referring to the erection of a
shrine.

The lower part of an altar, now lost, records HBAT, which has been
taken to refer to either a cohort of Batavians or Baetasians.

WESTERWOOD

The wife of a centurion of the Sixth Legion dedicated an altar here, suggesting
the presence of a detachment of the legion.

CROY HILL

Three building stones indicate work by the Sixth Legion, but an altar by a
member of the legion, together with the tombstone of a legionary, are more
indicative of occupation by a legionary detachment.

BAR HILL

*cohors I Baetasiorum quingenaria peditata civium Romanorum ob virtutem
et fidem*
The grandiloquent title records that the regiment had been granted Roman
citizenship for valour and loyalty. It was originally raised in Lower Germany
(modern Netherlands) after the Civil War of 68/9 and sent to Britain. It is
attested at Bar Hill, where it is recorded building, and at Old Kilpatrick. After
the abandonment of the Antonine Wall, it moved to Maryport.

cohors I Hamiorum quingenaria peditata
Originally raised in Syria, it may have formed part of the invasion army of 43.
Under Hadrian, it was at Carvoran on Hadrian's Wall, returning there after
the abandonment of the Antonine Wall. The names of two of its prefects,
Caristanius Iustianus, and Gaius Iulius Marcellinus, who died at the fort, are
known. Tanicius Verus may have been commander of the unit here rather than
that at Cadder to which he is sometimes assigned.

The site has produced a building record of a detachment of the Second
and Twentieth Legions and a second by a detachment, possibly of the same
legions.

AUCHENDAVY
Four altars dedicated by Cocceius Firmus, centurion of the Second Legion,
together with a building stone and two tombstones of soldiers of the legion,
suggest that a detachment of that legion was based here. A fragmentary stone
appears to be a dedication by soldiers of the same legion and a cavalry
regiment.

KIRKINTILLOCH
No evidence for a garrison.

CADDER
No unit is known here, but the fort is of a size to hold a *cohors quingenaria
peditata*. Tanicius Verus may have commanded here rather than at Bar Hill. A
fragment of a building stone of the Second Legion is also known.

BALMUILDY
No unit is known here, but the fort is of a size to hold a *cohors quingenaria
peditata*. Caecilius Nepos, tribune, is recorded on an altar. Two stones record
the Second Legion building here under Lollius Urbicus.

BEARSDEN
No unit is attested here, but the fort appears to contain cavalry barrack-
blocks. A building stone records work by the Twentieth Legion.

CASTLEHILL
cohors IV Gallorum quingenaria equitata
This regiment, originally raised in France, may have been part of the invasion
force. It is recorded at Castlesteads on Hadrian's Wall, Risingham, in the later
second century and Vindolanda in the third and fourth century. When at
Castlehill, its commander, Pisentius Iustus dedicated an altar to the Goddesses
of the Parade-ground.

Duntocher

No unit recorded: the fort is too small to have held a complete unit.

Old Kilpatrick

cohors I Baetasiorum quingenaria peditata civium Romanorum

See under Bar Hill. While at Old Kilpatrick it dedicated an altar to Jupiter. Its commanding officer at that time was Publicius Maternus but Iulius Candidus, a centurion of the First Italian Legion, was acting on his behalf. This legion was normally based on the Lower Danube, and it is difficult to envisage the circumstances which led to Iulius Candidus being present on the British frontier almost at the other end of the empire. Eric Birley proposed that Candidus came with the expeditionary force led by the Emperor Septimius Severus in the early third century, but we have no evidence that Old Kilpatrick was occupied at this time. Roy Davies suggested that the centurion might have travelled with Statius Priscus in 161/2. Priscus, though, was governor of Upper Moesia, whereas the First Italian Legion was based in Lower Moesia. I have argued that the officer was recording his new appointment to which he was about to move. In such cases, however, the existing post is usually recorded as well as the new position. Finally, Vivien Swan has argued that Candidus helped supervise the transfer of the British army back from Mauretania about 150. Lawrence Keppie has suggested the unusual appointment might indicate that the cohort was divided between Old Kilpatrick and Bar Hill.

APPENDIX II

THE ROMAN NAMES OF THE FORTS ON THE ANTONINE WALL

The *Ravenna Cosmography* lists a number of sites which have been taken to be forts along the Antonine Wall. The heading of the section is: 'there are places in Britain itself, connected with each other in a straight line from one part to the other, where Britain itself is most narrow from ocean to ocean, these are: *Velunia, Volitanio, Pexa, Begesse, Colicana, Medio Nemeton, Subdobiadon, Litana, Cibra* and *Credigone*'.

Unfortunately, there are only ten names and at least seventeen forts known on the line of the Wall. The inscription found in 1956 at Carriden confirms that the fort at the eastern end of the Wall was *Velunia*. *Medio Nemeton* (or *Medionemeton*) has been identified as Cairnpapple, a religious site in the Bathgate Hills which was in use over several centuries up to the Early Christian period, and as the Roman temple at Arthur's O'on.

It has been suggested that the ten names relate to the ten forts which were larger than 0.7 ha (2 acres): Carriden, Mumrills, Castlecary, Bar Hill, Auchendavy, Cadder, Balmuildy, Bearsden, Castlehill and Old Kilpatrick. An alternative proposal is that the *Ravenna Cosmography* only lists the forts held later in the second century.

APPENDIX III

THE GOVERNERS OF BRITAIN DURING THE OCCUPATION OF THE ANTONINE WALL

QUINTUS LOLLIUS URBICUS 139–42
Born at Cirta (Constantine) in north Africa. His military service included: tribune of legion XXII Primigenia in Upper Germany; commander of legion X Gemina at Vienna in Upper Pannonia (modern Austria); service in the Jewish war of 132–5; governor of Lower Germany and then Britain. He was clearly sent to undertake the invasion of southern Scotland, and is recorded on two inscriptions on the Antonine Wall. In the 150s Urbicus was prefect of the city of Rome.

UNKNOWN, PERHAPS CORNELIUS PRISCIANUS 142/3–44?
The name of a governor was erased from the Ingliston milestone. The consular date on the milestone is either II or [I]II. Antoninus was consul for the third time in 140 and the milestone cannot date to 139 for Urbicus was then governor and was not subsequently damned with his name being removed from inscriptions. The milestone therefore dates to 143 or 144. In 145 a certain Cornelius Priscianus was condemned by the senate when he was governor of Spain, and he may have been the governor on the milestone.

CNAEUS PAPIRIUS AELIANUS 146
Aelianus is recorded as governor of Britain on a diploma dating to 146. He is probably the same man who had previously been governor of Upper Dacia (modern Romania).

CNAEUS IULIUS VERUS 158
Verus came from Aequum in Dalmatia. He was probably the son of Sextus Julius Severus, governor of Britain in the early 130s before moving to Judaea

to quell the rebellion there. He had served as a tribune in legion X Fretensis, commander of legion XXX Ulpia Victrix in Lower Germany, governor of the same province, and then of Britain, before moving on to be governor of Syria. He is recorded on an inscription from Birrens as being governor in 158. He also appears on the Ravenglass diploma which dates to 27 February 158 which therefore implies that he had arrived in Britain at least in the previous year.

...]anus 154 or 159
This fragmentary name is recorded on the Colchester diploma which probably dates to either 154 or 159.

Marcus Statius Priscus 162
Priscus started his career as commander of the fourth cohort of Lingones in Britain. He was then, unusually, tribune in three different legions and it was while holding one of these posts that he was decorated for service in the Jewish war of 132–5. He also served as commander of a cavalry unit in the eastern province of Cappadocia. Following his elevation to the senate, he was commander of legion XIV Gemina at Carnuntum in Upper Pannonia, governor of Dacia, governor of Upper Moesia and then Britain, before moving on to Cappadocia, where he led the Roman defence against the recent Parthian invasion. In between these military appointments he held several civil posts. He was probably in his early fifties when governor of Britain, an unusually late age, but clearly a very experienced general and administrator.

Sextus Calpurnius Agricola 163–5/6?
Nothing is known of Agricola's origins. The *Historia Augusta* records that he was sent to Britain by the new emperors, Lucius Verus and Marcus Aurelius, shortly after their accession in 161. He is recorded at Carvoran, Corbridge, Vindolanda and Ribchester. Following his governorship, Agricola moved to the Danube to participate in the warfare there.

APPENDIX IV

AFRICANS ON THE ANTONINE WALL?

In examining the pottery from Bearsden, Vivien Swan realised that some was made in a style used in cooking in an African manner, that is that the pots were made to stand on a little brazier: part of at least one brazier was found at Bearsden. Similar pots were then recognised by her at eight or nine other forts along the Wall, mostly towards its west end. The challenge was then to determine how African cooking styles, leading to the local production of pottery in an African style, came to be introduced to the Antonine Wall.

Opportunities for links between the Antonine Wall and Africa were few. Certainly, Lollius Urbicus came from Africa, but one man, and in his position, is hardly likely to have introduced a new style of cooking to north Britain. Soldiers for the British army were not recruited in Africa, and troops movements are unknown, with one exception. The Mauretanian War of Antoninus Pius was so serious, as we have seen, that it led to reinforcements being sent from many provinces. An inscription from Rome records the career of Sextus Flavius Quietus: *primus pilus*, that is first centurion, of legion XX Valeria Victrix; sent by the Emperor Antoninus Pius with an expeditionary force against the Moors; prefect of the British fleet. It has been suggested that Quietus led the expeditionary force while first centurion of the Second Legion, but that is most unlikely. After holding the post of *primus pilus* in the Second Legion for a year, he would have been transferred to Rome where he would have been available for special duties, in his case the command of the expeditionary force to north Africa.

The career of Sextus Flavius Quietus, therefore, provides no independent support for the participation of British troops in the Moorish War of Antoninus. Such participation, however, remains the best way of explaining the appearance of African cooking styles in Britain. British troops serving in Africa could have either have adopted African cooking styles, acquired some African slaves (a Moorish freedman, Victor, died and was buried at South

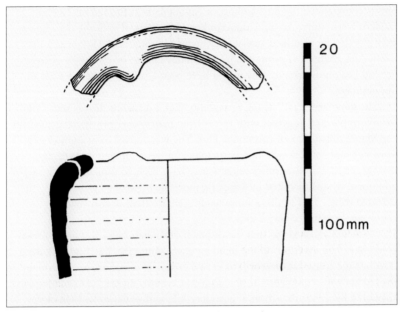

Fig. A.1 Drawing of a brazier for cooking, found at Bearsden.

Shields), recruited some local men into their units, or even been assigned some
new recruits from amongst the defeated tribes, a common occurrence. Groups
of Moors appear at forts in Dacia (modern Romania) and Upper Moesia
(Serbia) in 158–61. A *numerus Maurorum Aurelianorum* is attested at Burgh-
by-Sands on Hadrian's Wall a hundred years later, but there is the strong
possibility that it was already at the fort towards the end of the second
century. This regiment, therefore, may have come to Britain in the aftermath of
Antoninus' Mauretanian War. A parallel may be drawn with the peace treaty
agreed between Marcus Aurelius, the successor of Antoninus, and the
Marcomani and Quadi in 175. These two German states had to contribute
8,000 cavalry to the Roman army, of which 5,500 were sent to Britain. Only
one *ala Sarmatorum* is attested in Britain and it seems that the remaining
soldiers were spread amongst other units.

One possible member of the putative detachment sent to Africa may be
identified. The 1000-strong First Cohort of Vardullians, later stationed at
Castlecary on the Antonine Wall, appears to have been reduced in strength.
The main evidence is the use of prefect as the title of the commanding officer
rather than tribune which was appropriate for a unit of this size. This suggests
that part of the unit was absent. Moreover, one prefect of the regiment, named
Sittius, was a native of Cirta in modern Algeria, reinforcing the link: another

Sittius commanded the First Cohort of Aquitanians at Brough-on-Noe in modern Derbyshire. An individual soldier who returned with the detachment may possibly be identified as Caius Octavius Honoratus of Thuburnica in north Africa who was promoted by Antoninus Pius to be centurion of the Second Legion in Britain. This would have been a suitable time for such an appointment.

In summary, it is a strong probability that a detachment was sent from Britain to partake, together with forces from many other provincial armies, in the Mauretanian War of Antoninus Pius. The war started in or immediately after 145 and soldiers who had participated in the campaign were being discharged in 150. Returning soldiers may have been accompanied by additional troops recruited in Africa or, more likely, soldiers provided by the defeated tribes. This is also a more likely scenario than British soldiers acquiring African cooking habits.

Vivien Swan realised that the dispatch of soldiers from Britain to Africa could have had an effect on the building of the Antonine Wall and a slowing down of the construction work, or even a complete cessation, could explain the late date for completion of the project. Certainly an unusual situation is suggested by the construction of a pottery kiln within the stoke-hole of the bath-house within the fort at Bar Hill. The use of the furnace in this way can only mean that the bath-house was not in use, which in turn implies that the unit was absent from the fort. Of particular interest is that the pottery made in the kiln placed in the furnace was in an African style. It may not be too fanciful to suggest that, after a period of abandonment, or greatly reduced occupation, new soldiers arrived, fresh from north Africa, and made themselves some new pottery before they brought the bath-house back into its more normal use. The significance of the African-style cooking wares on the Antonine Wall and their implications for the building programme are taken into account in the relevant chapters of this book.

APPENDIX V

WHERE TO SEE THE ANTONINE WALL

Rampart and ditch
Rough Castle to the east of Bonnybridge and Seabegs Wood to the west.

Rampart base
New Kilpatrick Cemetery, Bearsden; Golden Hill, Duntocher.

Ditch
Polmont; Watling Lodge, Falkirk – Rough Castle, Bonnybridge; Castlecary – Twechar; Iain Road, Bearsden.

Military Way
Rough Castle, with quarry pits preserved between the Military Way and the access track in the western sector; Seabegs Wood.

Distance slab
A replica of the text of the Bridgeness distance slab stands in the wall beside the Bridgeness Tower in Bo'ness.

Forts
Rough Castle, Bonnybridge: here the earthworks of the fort, its annexe and a possible fortlet are visible.
Bar Hill, Twechar: the platform of the fort is discernible, together with the east gate and its outer protecting ditch; within, the headquarters building and bath-house are exposed.
Castlecary: the fort platform, crossed by the railway, can be traced. Some stones of the east fort wall north of the railway and of the headquarters building can be seen.
Croy Hill: nothing is visible, though the location of the fort can be determined

Fig. A.2 The bath-house at Bar Hill.

Fig. A.3 The bath-house and latrine at Bearsden.

from the ruined farmhouse and clump of trees on the site. A few metres to the east, a section of the ditch is uncut.

Westerwood: the hollows of the fort ditches on the west and south sides may be seen.

Duntocher: the site of the fort is on publicly owned land, but is not visible.

Bath-houses
Bar Hill and Bearsden.

Fortlet
Kinneil, Bo'ness: the museum beside Kinneil Palace contains finds from the fortlet.
Croy Hill: the platform on which the fortlet sits lies west of the fort.

'Expansions'
Rough Castle, Bonnybridge: the visible 'expansion' lies to the left of the entrance to the site. The other three 'expansions' at Rough Castle are also visible but are not on publicly owned land.
Croy Hill: two 'expansions' stand on the west brow of the hill.

Museums
Museum of Scotland, Chambers Street, Edinburgh.
Hunterian Museum, University Avenue, Glasgow.
Auld Kirk Museum, Kirkintilloch.
Kinneil Museum, Bo'ness.

A TOUR ALONG THE ANTONINE WALL

Those sections of the Wall in public ownership are marked in italics.

The west end of the Antonine Wall is now lost, but lies at Ferrydyke, close to the canal bridge on Portpatrick Road in **Old Kilpatrick**; a distance slab was found here. The site of the fort is now mostly occupied by the former bus garage as well as houses in Gavinburn Gardens.

The Wall, crossed and obliterated by the railway and A82, turns towards the east on the north side of the dual carriageway, its line being marked by the farm of Mount Pleasant and the gas governor kiosk. The land rises to the north towards the Kilpatrick Hills. The Wall passes to the north of the cemetery and then takes the line of the track past the school and Beeches Road running through **Duntocher**. Golden Hill, now a public park, was the site of the fort (*West Dunbartonshire*). A section of stone base, crossed by a culvert, is visible on the western slope of the hill.

The Wall disappears under housing, but across the A810 its line is adopted by the track leading to Cleddans farm. The ditch now becomes faintly visible down to the burn, across Hutcheson Hill (*East Dunbartonshire*) and, after crossing Peel Glen Road, as it climbs the prominent knoll known as Castlehill with its circle of trees. Once the site of a fort, it is equally important as a marker for the Wall. To its east, an open strip of ground is signposted as the line of the Wall, though again it is mostly lost under houses. A short length of ditch in Roman Park can be accessed from Iain Road, Milverton Avenue and Westbourne Crescent (*East Dunbartonshire*).

Roman Road, leading east from **Bearsden Cross**, sits on the Military Way. The bath-house beside the fort is signposted (*Historic Scotland*), and the west ditches of the fort are marked by a slight hollow in the modern road. Next to the bath-house is part of an earlier bath building, a latrine and the east rampart of the annexe. The building of the railway forced a re-alignment of Roman Road, which crosses the A81 and climbs the hill towards **New Kilpatrick Cemetery** (*East Dunbartonshire*) where two lengths of rampart base are exposed. The ditch is also visible to the west of the cemetery and accessed through a gate.

The Wall, criss-crossing the modern roads, is ploughed flat from here to Balmuildy, though its location has often been revealed through excavation. In the absence of a strong linear element to the landscape, it moves from high point to high point, changing direction, for example, within the cemetery and on the summit of Crow Hill to the south of the B8049. A short length of rampart has been reconstructed in the garden centre.

The fort of **Balmuildy** sits on the plateau to the south of the River Kelvin, on the farm of that name, beside the A879. The minor road running east from the fort follows the line of the Wall until it turns sharp south towards Bishopbriggs and the A803; a short length of ditch is visible at one kink in the road. The Wall continues easterly across Cawder golf course towards the site of the fort at Cadder, now destroyed. At the roundabout where the A807 and A803 meet to the east of Cadder, the belt of trees to the west marks the Wall. From the roundabout and running eastwards, the A803 is at first immediately north of the road, and then, from Glasgow Bridge, to the south. Peel Park in **Kirkintilloch** occupies the site of the fort (*East Dunbartonshire*).

At the east end of Kirkintilloch, the Wall survives as open space to the north of the 1960s' housing from St Flannan's Church, Hillhead, eastwards until it runs under the canal (*Historic Scotland*) just to the east of Inchbelly Bridge. The B8023 occupies the site of the Military Way as it passes through **Auchendavy** fort, now occupied by a farm; the eastern ditches are faintly visible. The modern road from here to Twechar roughly follows the line of the Wall.

A few metres south of the canal bridge in **Twechar**, the ditch is clearly visible to the east of the road, though clogged with trees and bushes. Access is

Fig. A.4 The distance slab found at the west end of the Antonine Wall.

achieved by way of the signposted access track beside the war memorial. This leads to **Bar Hill** fort (*Historic Scotland*). The platform of the fort may be discerned and within it the headquarters building and bath-house have been consolidated. The drain at the north-east corner and the east entrance are also visible; the latter had special protection in the form of a ditch. The rocky knoll to the east of the fort appears to have been an Iron Age fort; the shelving slope to the north indicates the former position of its ramparts. The Antonine Wall ditch curves round the north side of the hill-fort, but was not always completed by the Roman army. At the top of the slope, north of the hill-fort, it was not excavated. Beyond that is a stretch from which the top soil has been removed, then more soil before it achieves its full depth. There follows a spectacular section of ditch.

At the end of the walk, a track leads through the forestry plantation towards Croy, the track soon returning to the line of the Wall, with the ditch faintly visible to the north of the track. Signposts and gates allow walkers to continue across the fields along the north side of Croy village towards **Croy Hill** (*Historic Scotland*). On the west brow of the hill are two 'expansions' with the rampart visible between the pair. But it is the ditch which is the most remarkable feature over the hill. It is cut where clearly unnecessary, at first within the natural trough to the north of the Wall and then running along the foot of the crags, sometimes 30 m (100 ft) from the rampart. On the east side of the hill a small group of trees occupies the site of the fort; a fortlet lay on the platform to the west.

At the disused railway line, the Wall, with the ditch still visible, continues straight on, but the path turns north along the track and onto the modern road. A detour to the south following the road leads to the next visible stretch, signposted from the road along the track past Easter Dullatur farm. The track lies beside the Wall, which is crossed by the railway at an oblique angle. To the south of the bridge under the railway (*Historic Scotland*) the ditch re-appears. Now begins a 5 km (3 mile) stretch throughout most of which the ditch is clearly visible. The track lies on the upcast mound, then in the ditch through the golf course, until the buildings of the former **Westerwood** farm. This lies within a small fort, of which only the slight hollow of the ditches is visible to the south and west. The track continues along the north side of Cumbernauld airfield. Here a fine line of trees at **Tollpark** (*Historic Scotland*) occupies the upcast mound and leads, across Wyndford Road at Garnhall, on to **Castlecary** (*Historic Scotland/North Lanarkshire*).

The path ends behind Castlecary Hotel. The A80 then has to be negotiated. On the eastern side sits the fort at **Castlecary** (*Historic Scotland*). Bisected by the railway, some stones are visible to the north, including the outer face of the east wall and the rear of the headquarters building. The B816 lies to the south of the Wall, whose ditch is intermittently visible through Allandale. **Seabegs Wood** (*Historic Scotland/NTS*) has sat within its boundaries since at least 1787. A fine stretch of rampart, ditch and upcast mound run through the wood and by its south boundary is the Military Way. At the western end of the wood, the ditch bends north to embrace the fortlet which sat on the nose of land to the west.

The Wall and Military Way continue through the wood to the stream. Beyond, the south slope of the ditch may be observed on the south side of the road. The Wall and modern road then diverge, the Wall passing under the houses of Seabegs. It crosses the B816 linking Bonnybridge and High Bonnybridge beside Antonine Primary School. Here, the medieval Seabegs Motte sits on the upcast mound to the north of the ditch.

Rough Castle (*Historic Scotland/NTS*) is accessed from Bonnybridge along a minor road which eventually turns into a track. Where the track turns left, it crosses the ditch, which approaches from the right past the knoll known as Elf Hill. The rampart on the left lies in the wooded policies of Bonnybridge House: here is an 'expansion'. The next stretch of Wall is perhaps the most remarkable along the whole line of the Wall. The rampart, ditch and upcast mound are all visible. The Military Way at first lies under the track, but then emerges as a distinct mound. Between the track and the rampart are small hollows: the quarry pits from which gravel was extracted to use in the Military Way. The second 'expansion' of the pair lies just to the west of the cattle grid.

The Rowan Tree Burn crosses the site and beyond is the fort of Rough Castle. This was one of the smallest forts on the Wall, but the defences are visible round all sides. An additional outer ditch protects the western flank. To the north, a series of defensive pits are exposed. To the east of the fort is an annexe, crossed by the Military Way. To the east of the fort and north of the Military Way, a shallow ditch may mark the site of an earlier fortlet.

The rampart, ditch and upcast mound can be followed through Tentfield Plantation, as can the Military Way, though with less facility. An 'expansion' lies a little to the east of the line of the former railway with its pair almost at the east end of the wood. To the east of Lime Road, the ditch can be observed in ground owned by Falkirk Council. Where the modern road crosses the Wall is a stretch in state care. The second sector to the east of **Watling Lodge** (*Historic Scotland/NTS*) retains the ditch at almost its original dimensions.

The Wall is not visible through Falkirk, except at **Bantaskine** (*Historic Scotland*), where the ditch is well preserved, and Kemper Avenue (*Falkirk*), where a short length of the rampart lies at the south of the car park. In between, the Wall lies to the south of the historic centre of Falkirk, following Arnothill towards the Pleasance, the site of the fort. The ditch is visible through most of Callendar Park (*Falkirk*). Beyond the railway at the east end of the park, Grahamsdyke Street in Laurieston lies on the Wall as far as Mumrills, beyond which the hollow occupied by the blocked-off road is the Wall ditch. Modern roads have obscured its line, though it follows the link road to the motorway, and then heads for the twin spires of Polmont Church, destroyed by the motorway which crosses the Wall obliquely. Beyond Polmont, a good stretch of ditch is visible in **Millhall Wood** (*Falkirk*) and then, after the golf course, beside the ski-slope (*Falkirk*).

Here the Wall crosses the River Avon, protected by a fort, and climbs the slope beyond. From **Inveravon** farm the minor road lies in the ditch overlooking the vast petrochemical works of Grangemouth, all built on land reclaimed from the sea since Roman times. At the T-junction the road turns north to drop down to circle round the park at **Kinneil** (*Falkirk*), which is best approached from the east. Within the park a fortlet has been exposed and laid open for inspection; the only one to be seen on the Wall. The ramparts, gates and internal buildings are marked out; a secondary drain has removed the evidence for the posts on one side of the north gate.

Kinneil House sits on top of the Wall. The ditch is visible on the west bank of the Dean Burn at the east end of the drive. The Wall then follows the line of the modern road, Dean Road later becoming Grahamsyke Road. Towards the east end of Bo'ness, the Wall is traditionally believed to have plunged down to the Forth along Grahamsdyke Lane, but it has not been located here. In the wall beside **Bridgeness Tower** is a replica of the inscription on the distance slab found at the site in 1868 and probably marking the eastern end of the Antonine Wall.

Further Reading

The Antonine Wall

Bailey, G. B., *The Antonine Wall: Rome's Northern Frontier* (Falkirk, 2003)

Hanson, W. S., and Maxwell, G. S., *The Antonine Wall* (Edinburgh, 1986)

Hassall, M., 'The building of the Antonine Wall', *Britannia* 14 (1983) 262–4

Keppie, L., *Roman Inscribed and Sculptured Stones in the Hunterian Museum, University of Glasgow* (London, 1998)

Macdonald, G., *The Roman Wall in Scotland* (London, 1934)

Robertson, A. S., revised by Keppie, L., *The Antonine Wall* (Glasgow, 2001)

Roy, W., *The Military Antiquities of the Romans in Britain* (London, 1793)

Skinner, D. N., *The Countryside of the Antonine Wall* (Perth, 1973)

Tipping, R., 'The form and fate of Scottish woodlands', *Proceedings of the Society of Antiquaries of Scotland* 124 (1994), 1–54

Tipping, R. and Tisdall. E., 'The landscape context of the Antonine Wall: a review of the evidence', *Proceedings of the Society of Antiquaries of Scotland* 135 (2005) forthcoming

Woolliscroft, D. J., 'Signalling and the Design of the Antonine Wall', *Britannia* 27 (1996), 153–77

Lawrence Keppie's latest revision of *The Antonine Wall: a Hand-book to the Surviving Remains* (Glasgow 2001) contains a full bibliography which should be consulted for detailed references. The following articles have been published in the last five years:

Abdy, R.,'A survey of the coin finds from the Antonine Wall', *Britannia* 33 (2002), 189–217

Bailey, G.,'Excavations on the Roman temporary camps at the Three Bridges, Camelon, Falkirk', *Proceedings of the Society of Antiquaries of Scotland* 130 (2000), 469–90

Dunwell, A., Bailey, G., Leslie, A., and Smith, A., 'Some excavations on the line of the Antonine Wall, 1994–2001', *Proceedings of the Society of Antiquaries of Scotland* 132 (2002), 259–304

Glendinning, B., 'Investigations of the Antonine Wall and medieval settlement at Kinneil House, Bo'ness, Falkirk', *Proceedings of the Society of Antiquaries of Scotland* 130 (2000), 509–24

Hunter, F., 'Unpublished Roman finds from the Falkirk area', *Calatria* 15 (Autumn 2001), 111–23

Jones, R. 'Temporary camps on the Antonine Wall', *Limes XIX* (Pécs, 2005), 551–60

Keppie, L., 'New light on excavations at Bar Hill Roman fort on the Antonine Wall, 1902–05', *Scottish Archaeological Journal* 24.1 (March 2002), 21–48

Keppie, L., 'A walk along the Antonine Wall in 1825: the travel journal of the Rev John Skinner', *Proceedings of the Society of Antiquaries of Scotland* 133 (2003), 205–44

Keppie, L., 'A Roman bath-house at Duntocher on the Antonine Wall', *Britannia* 35 (2004), 179–224

Linge, J., 'The Cinderella Service: the Ordnance Survey and the mapping of the Antonine Wall', *Proceedings of the Society of Antiquaries of Scotland* 134 (2004), 161–71

Swan, Vivien G., 'The Twentieth Legion and the history of the Antonine Wall reconsidered', *Proceedings of the Society of Antiquaries of Scotland* 129 (1999), 399–480

THE ROMANS IN SCOTLAND

Breeze, D. J., *Roman Scotland: Frontier Country* (London, 2006)

Keppie, Lawrence, *The Legacy of Rome: Scotland's Roman Remains* (Edinburgh, 2004)

Maxwell, G. S., *The Romans in Scotland* (Edinburgh, 1998)

ROMAN BRITAIN

Breeze, D. J. and Dobson, B., *Hadrian's Wall* (London, 2000)

Frere, S. S., *Britannia* (London, 1987)

Holder, P. A., *The Roman Army in Britain* (London, 1982)

Salway, P., *Roman Britain* (Oxford, 1981)

ROMAN FRONTIERS

Luttwak, E. N., *The Grand Strategy of the Roman Empire from the First Century A.D. to the Third* (Baltimore and London, 1976)

Mattern, S. P., *Rome and the Enemy* (Berkley/Los Angeles/London, 1999)

Whittaker, C. R., *Frontiers of the Roman Empire, A Social and Economic Study* (Baltimore and London, 1994).

ANTONINUS PIUS

'Antoninus Pius', *Lives of the Later Caesars* (= *Historia Augusta*), translated by Birley, A., (London, 1976)

Birley, A. R., *Marcus Aurelius* (London, 1987)

Birley, A. R., *Hadrian, the Restless Emperor* (London and New York, 1997)

Bryant, E. E., *The Reign of the Emperor Antoninus Pius* (Cambridge, 1895)

Hüttl, W., *Antoninus Pius* (Prague, 1933 and 1936)

INDEX

The page references for illustrations are marked in italic